Strategic Planning for Smaller Businesses

Strategic Planning for Smaller Businesses

Improving Corporate Performance and Personal Reward

David A. Curtis
David A. Curtis & Associates

LexingtonBooks
D.C. Heath and Company
Lexington, Massachusetts
Toronto

Library of Congress Cataloging in Publication Data

Curtis, David A. (David Arnold)
   Strategic planning for smaller businesses.

   Includes index.
   1. Corporate planning. 2. Small business—Planning. 3. Small
business—Management. I. Title.
HD30.28.C87   1983   658.4'012   82-48171
ISBN 0-669-09815-9 (pbk.)

Third printing, November 1984

Published simultaneously in Canada

Printed in the United States of America on acid-free paper

International Standard Book Number: 0-669-06011-9 Casebound

International Standard Book Number: 0-669-09815-9 Paperbound

Library of Congress Catalog Card Number: 82-48171

For Stephen and Helen, with love.

Contents

Figures

Tables

Preface and Acknowledgments

This book covers a conventional topic, strategic planning, from an unconventional viewpoint, that of the small-business person. Academics and staff planners at major corporations have developed an imposing array of planning tools for analyzing large businesses and developing effective strategies to guide them. Academics and venture capitalists have also developed a second set of tools, equally imposing, to identify and stimulate entrepreneurial activity so that small businesses can rapidly become large ones. Yet the vast majority of businesses in the United States and elsewhere are small businesses managed by one person or a small group determined to be successful despite the odds.

These people frequently dedicate all their assets, talents, and time to their businesses. What strategies are they using? Can the strategies be improved? Can the business be organized and operated so that it repays them fully? The assertion made in this book is that a properly formulated strategy can help a small business immensely. The rewards of small-business strategies to the owners and managers can go beyond sharing in the profits, to include pleasure from guiding the activities of a sound business and satisfaction from using the business as a vehicle to achieve personal objectives. In addition, the skills and experience developed during the strategic-planning process provide excellent insurance against unexpected changes in business conditions—the owners and managers know how to assess threats and opportunities, and how to change the business to meet the new conditions.

After seventeen years of consulting, it has become obvious to me that most of the strategic-planning techniques used to guide the affairs of large businesses are not appropriate for smaller businesses. Many such techniques cannot be used in smaller businesses at all because of differences in the scale of operations; few appear to account fully for the limited resources (including time) of the typical small business. None explicitly includes the personal characteristics of the important people in the business so that the strategy reflects their strengths and weaknesses and satisfies their personal needs and objectives. It seems only fair that the best small-business strategy should meet the personal requirements of the people who commit all their time and efforts to a business. I do not know of any large-business strategy that can provide this extra benefit.

This book describes an approach to strategic planning for smaller businesses that is based on extensive experience with strategic planning for large companies, modified by equally extensive experience in consulting for smaller companies in the United States, Japan, and western Europe. Many people have contributed, often unwittingly, to the development of these ideas. Only one can be mentioned here: my father, who ran a small business for almost fifty years, through good times and bad, working hard to make it grow, struggling with government regulations and rationing of products, and finally facing severe price competition from a much larger competitor. The concrete statement of the ideas presented here is a memorial to his hard work and unfailing guidance. I am grateful to him and to many others for their contributions to developing the techniques discussed in this book.

**Strategic
Planning
for Smaller
Businesses**

1 Introduction

"We must ask where we are and whither we are tending."
—Abraham Lincoln

Why Plan?

Plan is an emotional word for many people. Many opinions reflect the hopes, beliefs, experiences, and frustrations of anyone who has ever tried to plan, whether for a social event, a vacation, or a business. Many say, "I never plan; it's a waste of time." Yet, everyone has plans whether formally established or not. The same is true for owners and managers of businesses: they all have plans for their businesses. The plans differ in quality, not in whether they exist or not. The characteristics of poor business plans are that they are implicit, vague, and usually formed as a response to the complex, even messy, problems faced by executives. The choice is not whether to plan, but whether to plan effectively. Poor planning takes little effort and quickly verifies any preconceived notions that it is a waste of time by producing few positive results. Good planning attempts to apply well-tested problem-solving techniques to a business. It takes effort but it is usually rewarded by improvements in the business's performance and by the assurance that changes in the external business environment will not take the planner by surprise. In fact, the executive who learns to plan well develops a feeling of control of his or her business's destiny, in contrast to feeling at the mercy of events, or just going from crisis to crisis.

The planning process can have several other favorable impacts on the day-to-day operation of a business in addition to improving longer term performance and providing an improved feeling of well-being for the executives involved. For instance:

careful planning improves business decisions, highlighting the advantages in some alternatives and encouraging rejection of other opportunities that may be initially intriguing but which really would tie up business resources or time that could be better applied to the main activities of the business;

small changes in daily tasks can increase overall effectiveness considerably; and

1

the development of a business plan allows appropriate aspects of it to be communicated to other managers and employees in an understandable way so that they can participate more effectively in achieving the longer-term performance improvements and other objectives sought.

There are several barriers that tend to inhibit planning:

Time pressures (making the commitment of time to develop and maintain the plan).

Continuing commitment (maintaining the commitment to the chosen course of action and actually implementing the plan).

Reluctance to give up the alternative goals not chosen. The choice of one goal implicitly means that others have been rejected, so, unless the planning process has a mechanism for clearly establishing the superior value of the chosen goals, the rejected goals will be resurrected from time to time to interfere with the implementation of the main plan;

Fear of failure. If no goals are selected, then it is not possible to fail. Making a commitment to the future involves a risk to the planner's self-esteem if a goal is not achieved, so some people find it difficult to commit themselves to major goals.

Lack of knowledge about the true characteristics of the business. It is difficult to choose goals and make plans when you are not completely certain about the strengths and weaknesses of your business and the mechanisms by which it operates. Confusion about the current situation can lead to confusion about what the future goals should be.

Lack of knowledge about the environment in which the business operates. This lack of awareness can obscure threats to and opportunities for a business, making it more difficult to develop goals and plans to meet those goals.

Insecurity and low self-confidence of the planner. Executives who continually deal with crises and feel that they are the hopeless victims of circumstances have great difficulty committing themselves to future goals and developing the necessary plans. In order to make a commitment to a goal, it is necessary to believe that it is achievable, which, in business, implies a sense of self-control and control over aspects of the environment.

In spite of these barriers, the benefits of planning (enhanced understanding of the business and the environment in which it operates, a mechanism for communicating to others their roles in the business, guidelines for judging the performance of the business, guidelines for making day-to-day business decisions, greater satisfaction in operating the business, improved performance in many situations, and the ability to respond to change) make planning not just worthwhile but essential.

Why Strategic Planning?

What is Strategic Planning?

Many adjectives and modifiers can be applied to the noun *planning*—long-range, product, budget, affirmative-action, and so on—but with few exceptions, their definitions are ambiguous. This is true for *strategic planning* also; there is no widely accepted definition, and certainly no succinct definition. A business-school definition relates strategic planning to the systematic development of a corporate strategy. Corporate strategy is systematic decision making in a company that determines objectives; establishes the principal policies and plans to achieve these goals; defines the business the company is in; the organization it is or wants to become; the returns it wishes to make to shareholders; and the contributions it intends to make to employees, customers, and the community. A shorter and more direct definition by Donald J. Taffi is, "[Strategic] planning attempts to identify the most effective means of deploying corporate resources in relation to the changing characteristics of one's business environment."[1] What is hidden behind these words? Charles Hofer and Dan Schendel provide a more vivid description of corporate strategy. They point out that businesses are started, operated, and liquidated, and that it is often difficult to determine why one business succeeds and another apparently similar business fails.[2] They appeal to a biological analogy—the survival of the fittest—to distinguish between continuing success and imminent or actual failure. The fittest businesses, that is the ones who continue to serve customers' needs profitably, survive. Unlike living organisms, a business can change its operations to respond to changes in the environment and so prolong its active life. These changes are the strategic decisions that a manager makes, and the process that identifies changes in the environment and the necessary business responses to these changes is called strategic planning. More directly stated, *strategic planning is the process by which a business prepares to maintain its competitiveness in the marketplace.* Because businesses have continuity, strategic planning is also a continuing process.

What are the Benefits of Strategic Planning?

Just as everyone has a business plan, varying in quality and explicitness, every business executive has a business strategy. The better strategies are those which are explicitly developed and reflect the peculiar needs of the business and the environment in which it operates. Every executive must continuously pay attention to the efficiency with which his or her business is operated; there are many benefits to be derived from increasing business efficiency including increased profits, potentially reduced costs, increased competitiveness, and better return on the investment made. However, effectiveness of operation, that is the extent to which a business produces desirable outputs, is also an important measure of competitiveness. No matter how efficiently a business produces its output, it will certainly fail if it is the wrong, ineffective output. An aphorism attributed to Peter Drucker highlights this dichotomy very well: he suggested that it is more important to do the right things [improve effectiveness] than to do things right [improve efficiency]. Strategic planning that identifies which outputs are or will be effective in the marketplace and relates them to the ability of the business to perform certain activities efficiently is essential to the business's continued survival. For example, a decade ago, manufacturers of slide rules were very efficient but obviously not very effective in meeting the competition from manufacturers of electronic calculators with slide-rule functions. This brought about a structural change in the industry and severe losses for several companies.

Why Should Executives Do Strategic Planning?

The most important reason why executives, that is the owners/Chief Executive Officers (owner/CEOs) and senior managers of a business responsible for its operations, should do strategic planning is its close relation to the survival of the business. It does not make sense to allow a company's best salesperson to develop product strategy by accepting every order with new product features even though no other customer may need them when they are developed and manufactured. Similarly, no matter how creative the new ideas from the staff, they may not lead to effective products valuable to customers. Also, lower managers often have limited perspective and strive to optimize efficiency to the exclusion of effectiveness.

Although many people at different levels in a business should be involved in the detailed preparation of the strategic plan, only the owner/CEOs have the business perspective, the ability to orchestrate a company's activities, the responsibility for setting objectives and the authority to review and change them, access to inputs from all internal and external sources, and the authority to resolve conflicts that arise during the planning process. They alone have available all the elements that must be molded into an effective business strategy. Owner/CEOs who do not participate actively in this process are tacitly conceding that there are aspects of their businesses that they find difficult to manage or influence significantly. They are abdicating responsibility for important decision making to others without the experience, overview, responsibility, or authority to make such decisions.

Business organizations can be modified to respond to changes in their efficiency and effectiveness and to actual or predicted changes in competition. These modifications require strategic planning to identify the most effective means to deploy a company's resources in relation to changes in the environment and competition. The plans, when developed, will facilitate informed decisions about changes in resources, improvements in efficiency, and improvements in effectiveness. Of course, the owner/CEO has many other responsibilities to discharge, and strategic planning must fit in with these, but it should not be neglected altogether since it is a form of insurance of the survival of the company.

Current Practice in Strategic Planning

Evolution of Strategic Planning

The concepts and application of strategic planning have only been explicitly recognized for about fifteen years. Before then, there was significant discussion of the importance and application of planning in business operations, especially long-range planning. Strategic planning has evolved from this earlier practice and long-range planning now supports the implementation of strategic plans. In 1958, Peter Drucker preferred to define long-range planning by what it does not do rather than by what it does.[3] He said that long-range planning is not forecasting since that requires predicting the future, which is only possible if the future evolves smoothly from the past. Forecasting of structural changes in an industry brought about by innovation is not possible. Long-range planning tries to compensate for this limitation in forecasting. Drucker also indicated that long-range planning is not about decisions to be made in the future; it is about current decisions in preparation for the future. It is ineffective to try to plan a decision to be made later. Finally, it is not an objective of long-range planning to eliminate risk. Instead, long-range planning prepares to take the correct risks. Stated positively, long-range planning as described by Drucker in the mid 1950s is making entrepreneurial (risk-oriented) decisions now, after due consideration of their impact, and organizing the company to implement them.

The seeds of a definition of strategic planning are contained in Drucker's description. However, there is no direct reference to modifying the business in response to actual or anticipated changes in the environment, and the competitive aspects of strategic planning are hidden in the use of the word *entrepreneurial*. It is currently recognized that forecasting can be a valuable management tool if it is used to restrict the ranges of variables included in a plan, not to define the variables precisely. Forecasting helps illuminate alternatives rather than specify one outcome.

Drucker discussed four trends that justify long-range planning and are also important reasons for performing strategic planning. In summary they are:

1. the time span over which business decisions retain their impact has lengthened, making systematic examination of the risks involved essential;
2. the rate at which innovations are being introduced, and the risks involved, are increasing rapidly;
3. the economy and business organizations are becoming more complex; and
4. employees in complex organizations need the guidance for making decisions provided by the long-range plan.

However, long-range planning was not universally adopted. A *Conference Board* publication in 1966 reported that more than 90 percent of 165 manufacturing firms responding to a survey engaged in long-range planning.[4] About one-third of the firms stated they applied long-range planning to almost all their activities while about half the firms only used it in some activities, usually finance, marketing, research and development, and capital budgeting. The overall impression given by the authors is that the techniques of long-range planning were ineffectively used. The main reasons given include insufficient commitment to planning by management; the pressure of daily duties; lack of perspective on the part of those who plan; communication, organization, and personnel problems; and various difficulties inherent in the planning process.

Even seven years later, there were critics of long-range planning, although by then the basic concepts of strategic planning were more widely known. In 1973 Harold Linstone wrote, "the planning staff is outside the mainstream of real decision-making."[5] In the same article, he lamented "Few managers ask . . . Do we want to control our own future or not?" Linstone advocated the benefits of long-range planning strongly. With the wisdom of hindsight, it is clear that the problems of long-range planning were with the planning tools as much as with the planners themselves. It is no wonder that more sophisticated tools such as those developed for strategic planning were introduced.

*The Application of Strategic Planning
by Major Corporations*

Today strategic planning is utilized by most major corporations and is generally recognized as a valuable technique. It is a set of tools developed by many practitioners over a period of fifteen years. Major contributions have come from academics, consultants, and corporate planners.

The first applications were to determine the best strategies to increase a market share and enhance product margins. The principal tools were cost analysis, value-added analysis, and experience-curve analysis. Cost analysis provided greater insight into the actual cost of manufacturing products or offering services, the cost of sales and distribution, and the cost of overhead. This allowed a company to determine which products were profitable and which were not. Value-added analysis showed executives which parts of their operations added the most value to their products and services and therefore contributed most to meeting overhead and earning profits. The experience curve was developed to allow planners to analyze the reduction in direct costs that usually occurs as the total production of a product increases. The cost reduction is attributed to improvements in worker efficiency as the manufacturing process becomes ingrained; improvements in the product design to facilitate its manufacture; and improvements in the manufacturing process that achieve the same result. A product with a large labor content typically has an experience factor of 80 percent; that is, the cost (in constant dollars) to manufacture the product declines by 20 percent every time the cumulative volume of production doubles (see figure 1-1).

In figure 1-1, the data are plotted on a logarithmic graph whose principal feature is that equal distances along each axis represent multiplication by a constant factor. The horizontal axis shows doubling of cumulative production at every scale, and the vertical axis shows increasing production cost by 1.25 times at every scale marker. The figure shows that manufacturing costs decrease with cumulative production.

The tools of cost, value-added, and experience-curve analysis were quickly generalized to include the operations of a multiproduct business whose products might not even be in similar markets. As a result, portfolio-management techniques were developed to optimize the corporation's performance perhaps at the expense of the performance of individual products. The portfolio-management technique looks at the future prospects, cash needs, and cash-producing capabilities of the different businesses in the company, where to stimulate growth, and how to finance it.

All of these techniques had as their goal the improvement of the corporation's performance both absolutely and with respect to the competitors; a process which requires detailed evaluation of the competitors and the environment in which the planner's company operates. New analytical techniques were also required to derive the greatest value from the data collected. It was quickly realized that a multibusiness corporation needed an overall corporate strategy within which the strategies of the component businesses could be developed. Within the general business strategy there are product strategies, marketing strategies, distribution strategies, and so

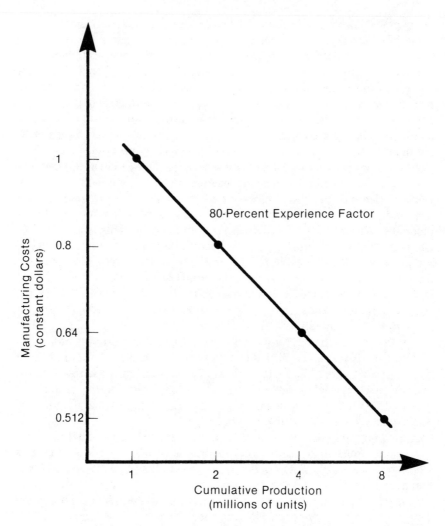

Figure 1-1. An Idealized Experience Curve

on. More recently, it was recognized that many of the engineering functions in a major business could benefit from strategic planning and now it is common to develop manufacturing strategies. The strength of the planning process comes from the integration of the strategic plans into a unified whole, cutting across boundaries inside and outside the company.

Even though there are now many commonly accepted principles of strategy planning and implementation, there is still room for individuality. General Electric Company, Inc., is known for the development of the strategic-business-unit concept (see chapters 4 and 5) and the application of business-attractiveness matrices for evaluating operations and opportunities (see figure 1-2). The matrix shows the position of two products manufactured by the planner's company, *P*1 and *P*2, and compares them with four other products, *A*1, *A*2, *B*1, and *C*2. The areas of the circles represent the relative market shares of each product. *A* competes with *P* in both product lines. *A* has a very small share of the market for product 2. *P* is in an excellent position in market 2 but lags behind *A* in market 1, competitively. *A* may have recently introduced an innovative new product. The matrix can also be used to represent the position of all of a company's products without showing the competitors by using circles whose areas represent the total size of the market for each product with a pie-slice-type shading to represent the company's share. These concepts were developed to help top executives maintain control over a major, rapidly growing, and diverse company.

The names of several major consulting firms are associated with major strategic-planning techniques although all large consulting firms probably use all the techniques as appropriate: Arthur D. Little's strategy centers, Booz, Allen & Hamilton's technology strategy, Boston Consulting Group's

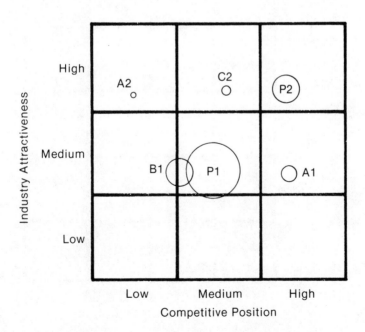

Figure 1-2. Business-Attractiveness Matrix (General Electric Co. Style)

market share/business portfolios, and McKinsey's competitive advantage are examples. The General Electric Co. and Arthur D. Little techniques both define businesses as activities with common strategies and provide ways to compare a number of businesses or products. Each technique plots businesses on a two-dimensional matrix with the strength of the business along one axis and the attractiveness of the industry along the other. Arthur D. Little uses an estimate of the maturity of the industry for the latter parameter, as in figure 1-3, while General Electric merges a number of con-siderations into its measurement of industry attractiveness. Only one com-pany can be dominant in a market, so in figure 1-3 only one circle can be plotted in the dominant row for each product, market, or industry under consideration. The three shaded areas in the bottom right corner of the plot represent business situations that are untenable and should be terminated as quickly as possible. Again, there are two possible presentations of the data: one showing competitors with the relative shares of the markets indicated by the areas of the circles; the other (shown in figure 1-3), showing all of

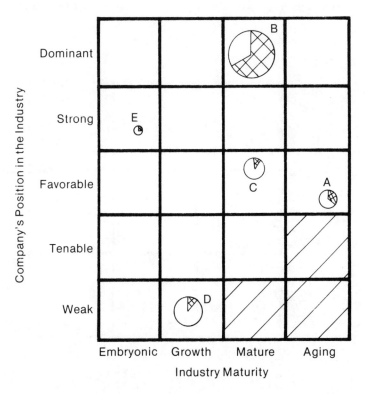

Figure 1-3. Business-Attractiveness Matrix (Arthur D. Little Style)

one company's products with the total market size indicated by the area of the circle and the company's share by the shaded area of the circle. Product *B* has a large share of a large but mature market in figure 1-3.

The Boston Consulting Group also uses a two-dimensional matrix to compare businesses, but this matrix uses the annual industry growth rate as a measure of business attractiveness and market share as a measure of the strength of the business (see figure 1-4). In figure 1-4, one company's products are plotted on the matrix. The areas of the circles represent the sales of each product. A product with a relative competitive position of 2 means that the company has twice the sales of the nearest competitor; while a product with a relative competitive position of 0.5 means that the sales are half those of the largest competitor.

McKinsey's competitive-advantage approach seeks to develop the strengths of a business and array them against the perceived weaknesses of the competition. Colloquially stated, they recommend that companies do not play in a game they are not sure they can win. Booz, Allen & Hamilton emphasize the need to include a company's technology strengths and weaknesses in the analyses that determine competitive position and business attractiveness.

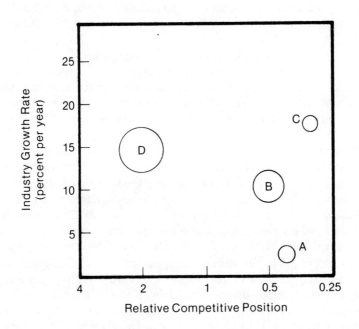

Note: Product A is in a very poor position

Figure 1-4. Business-Attractiveness Matrix (Boston Consulting Group Style)

Academic Work Underway

Academics are still researching many issues associated with management, including planning and performance. Among the objectives is a way to integrate those aspects of management which are now regarded as separate disciplines into a more general theory; for example the integration of organizational theory, human relations, and the competitive ability of corporations into a unified whole as attempted by William Ouchi.[6] However, there is still a lot of work to do and there are many conflicting approaches. On the one hand, in 1974 William Greenwood suggested that eleven management theories could be reduced to four major areas of theoretical activity.[7] On the other hand, Lawrence Mullins recently suggested that a broad threefold classification of management theory should be subdivided into eight parts.[8]

Two other active areas in the development of strategic-planning theory are the introduction of techniques for the explicit incorporation of technology in strategic planning, and further refinements of the techniques for quantifying subjective and qualitative variables such as customer preference so that rigorous analytic techniques can be used more extensively in strategic planning. In 1980, Alan Kantrow wrote, "The major unfinished business of the research literature is to provide managers with needed guidance in their formulation of a technological strategy for their companies."[9] An example of the continuing work to develop techniques for quantifying variables that appear to be inherently qualitative is an article on the psychology of preferences by Daniel Kahneman and Amos Tversky.[10] One area of business research that is not receiving the attention that it merits is small business. Albert Shapero of Ohio State University recently wrote that "influential forces in our society . . . consider small business . . . 'lowbrow.' "[11]

Of course, there are those who say that a too-strict adherence to the scientific method, with its emphasis on the development of hypotheses and their testing by analytical techniques, actually limits progress in the development of new insights, and in particular limits the exploration of new areas. The scientific method, according to this view, has difficulty developing hypotheses based on a proper review of complex situations.[12]

It is clear that we can expect further advances in the theory and application of strategic planning. But what about today's practitioner? If the theory is not fully developed, and if what is known is subject to argument, how can anyone develop strategic plans? Fortunately, the evidence is clear that the fundamental principles are known and that many companies, using pragmatic approaches, have developed effective strategic plans. Actually, strategic plans have existed for many years. The activities of the last fifteen years have increased the level of awareness of executives and planners of the value of planning rather than creating a whole new approach to planning. There is sufficient knowledge and experience with a range of proven planning techniques to provide a firm basis for the development of a strategic plan for any business.

Problems in Applying Strategic Planning to Smaller Businesses

The Different Characteristics of Smaller and Larger Businesses

There are many characteristics that distinguish small businesses from larger ones. An excellent appraisal of these differences is provided by John Welsh and Jerry White.[13] They emphasize that the difference between small and large businesses is not just one of scale in respect to numbers of employees, sales, assets, profits, and so on. They assert that a key issue in smaller businesses is the paucity of resources available to achieve objectives. Smaller businesses frequently cannot afford to hire the necessary specialized staff to perform accounting, personnel, or legal functions, and many smaller companies even have troubles meeting the fees of external professionals retained to perform these functions. The cost structure of a smaller business is also different from that of a larger business. It is not unusual to find that the owner/CEO's salary is the major payroll cost. The small size of the operation and the related small size of the resources leaves the business susceptible to even minor changes in the efficiency of its operations or to changes in the external environment. Changes in government regulations can have a major impact on small-business operating expenses. In contrast, large businesses operate in quasi-stable conditions when the size of the possible impact is measured against the size of the company's resources. The inertia of a large company enables it to smooth out many shocks that rock a small company dramatically, perhaps even causing critical damage. Another fact of life commonly faced by the smaller company is the frequency with which illogical competitors appear and disappear in their marketplace. Many managers, in one last desperate attempt to salvage a failing business, will cut prices excessively. Some newcomers even see this as a way to build revenues.

There are many lists cataloging the problems endemic to small businesses. The following is a composite list of the symptoms that most often lead to difficulties.

1. Lack of time
2. Lack of planning

3. Lack of attention to cash flow
4. Lack of working capital
5. Lack of financial controls
6. Lack of attention to return on investment
7. Lack of objectivity
8. Continuous crisis management
9. Inability of owner/CEO to delegate responsibility
10. Low employee morale
11. Poor work habits (owner/CEO and employees)
12. Low profits (poor sales, high costs, or both)
13. Chronic incidence of late shipments (lack of materials on hand, poor productivity, or poor scheduling)
14. Low inventory turnover
15. Poor communications (inside and outside the company)
16. Poor data concerning the business, the competition, the market, and technology changes
17. Poor pricing
18. Poor quality control in production
19. Too few employees
20. Failing to recognize the full impact of growth on overhead
21. Inadequate analysis of overhead, especially so-called fixed overhead
22. Gearing operations to the income statement to the exclusion of the balance sheet
23. Dependency on a single customer
24. Internal personality conflicts
25. Occasionally, the business grows beyond the capabilities of the owner/CEO

Similar lists can be prepared for major companies but such companies have the depth of experience and resources to live with many of the problems even if they are not eliminated. This highlights one of the most striking differences between the resources of the two classes of companies: executive time. The poverty of this resource in small companies is a major factor in determining what gets done and what does not get done. The owner/CEO of a smaller company has so many roles to play, including substituting for people who are unavoidably absent, that additional demands represent significant overloads and can not be handled.

Finally, the personal objectives of the people who can influence the business substantially are another difference between large and small businesses. Executives in major organizations are stewards of other people's investments and this must modify their objectives. In a small business, the owner/CEO can take whatever risks with the investment that seem appropriate, although there is usually a strong urge to be conservative and maintain the assets. Nevertheless, the assets frequently represent an extension of the owner/CEO, almost as a part of the person's personality and way of life. Owner/CEOs of smaller businesses frequently regard their businesses as the only way to achieve personal objectives as well as the only way to discharge their familial and social obligations. This is supported by their actual or perceived length of association with the business. For many it is a lifetime relationship and their businesses are their lives.

Many Strategic-Planning Tools Are
Inappropriate for Smaller Businesses

Many of the strategic-planning tools were developed for use by companies with several product lines or separate businesses—a situation not normally found among smaller companies. The portfolio-management technique is not obviously applicable to them, nor is the concept of strategic business units within one company. Other techniques take a macroscopic view of an industry and place the company under consideration in it. Many smaller companies get lost in these techniques; in fact, the uncertainty surrounding some of the data used is larger than the size of some of the companies concerned, calling the effectiveness of the whole strategic-planning process into question. Similarly, attempts to portray small companies in worldwide markets are frustrated by the mismatch of scales.

Other planning concepts need to be used carefully with smaller businesses, but they retain their validity. For example, the experience curve depicting the decrease in cost per unit manufactured as the cumulative volume increases does have meaning even on a small scale, but it is not reasonable to use it to compare the margins of a large and a small company. Also, the analysis of market share is viable as long as the market is correctly defined to account for the size of the competing businesses. Again, it does not usually make sense to mix large and small companies together in such an analysis.

Few strategic-planning tools can be directly applied to smaller businesses. Among those that can are competitive analysis, value-added analysis, cost analysis including direct and indirect costs, and competitive-advantage analysis. There do not seem to be any techniques that are only applicable to smaller companies.

Objectives of this Book

The principal objective of this book is to provide the owner/CEO (Chief Executive Officer) of a small business with a practical set of tools and techniques for strategic planning. These are derived from the best current practice in strategic planning for major corporations, but given an appropriate interpretation to account for the differences in the sizes of business. Where necessary, the techniques have been modified to suit the circumstances of smaller businesses. It is my intent to present this information in a straightforward way without recourse to lengthy definitions, complex theoretical arguments, or pages of numerical analysis. Executive time is precious in a small business and the most powerful tools will not be used if they take so much time and effort that the company's operations are interrupted or even stopped. A second objective is to encourage owner/CEOs to think systematically about their businesses so that strategic planning becomes a continuous process.

The definition of a small business used in this book is adapted from one proposed by the British Institute of Management: small businesses are those that are managed as such. In fact, the small business could be independently owned and operated, a subsidiary of another company with reasonable autonomy, or an autonomous division of a larger company. The significance of the definition lies in its reference to the characteristic style brought about by dominance of the owner/CEO in the affairs of the business, the special relationship between the owner/CEO and the business, and the existence of some degree of resource poverty.

The book is divided into nine chapters. Chapter 2 provides an overview of the strategic-planning process; chapter 3 covers the important issue of selecting objectives; chapter 4 gives examples of strategies; chapter 5 discusses the formulation of alternative strategies; chapter 6 concentrates on evaluation techniques and the selection of an appropriate strategy; chapter 7 addresses the planning steps necessary to convert strategy into implementable actions; chapter 8 continues the discussion of implementation with cautions concerning the possibility that the strategy may take on a life of its own, or that the existing implicit strategy is too well entrenched to be easily dislodged; and the final chapter presents a summary emphasizing the key points of the book. The reader with limited time may like to read chapters 2 and 9 first, and then read sections of the other chapters as appropriate when time becomes available.

Notes

1. Donald J. Taffi, *The Entrepreneur: A Corporate Strategy for the '80s* (New York: AMACOM, 1981), p. 20.

2. Charles W. Hofer and Dan Schendel, *Strategy Formulation: Analytical Concepts* (St. Paul, Minn.: West Publishing Company, 1978), p. 1.

3. Peter F. Drucker, "Long-Range Planning, Challenge to Management Science," *Management Science* 5 (April 1959):1-11.

4. James K. Brown, Saul S. Sands, and G. Clark Thompson, "The Status of Long-Range Planning," *The Conference Board Record* (September 1966):7-17.

5. Harold A. Linstone, "Planning: Toy or Tool?" *IEEE Spectrum* 10 (March 1973):62-71.

6. William Ouchi, *Theory Z* (Reading, Mass.: Addison-Wesley Publishing Company, 1981) pp. 97-160.

7. William T. Greenwood, "Future Management Theory: A 'Comparative' Evolution to a General Theory," *Academy of Management Journal* 17 (1974):503-513.

8. Lawrence Mullins, "Approaches to Management," *Management Accounting* 57 (1979):15-18.

9. Alan M. Kantrow, "The Strategy-Technology Connection," *Harvard Business Review* 58 (July-August 1980):6-21.

10. Daniel Kahneman and Amos Tversky, "The Psychology of Preferences," *Scientific American* 246 (January 1982):160-173.

11. Albert Shapero, "Why Don't Your Kids Want to be Entrepreneurs," *Inc.* 3 (September 1981):13-14.

12. Bela Gold, *Productivity, Technology, and Capital* (Lexington, Mass.: D.C. Heath LexingtonBooks, 1979), p. 9.

13. John A. Welsh and Jerry F. White, "A Small Business Is Not a Little Business," *Harvard Business Review* 59 (July-August 1981):18-32.

2

Overview of Strategic Planning for Smaller Businesses

"If we are to achieve results never before accomplished, we must expect to employ methods never before attempted." —Sir Francis Bacon

Management and Planning

A general definition of management is *organizing resources to meet objectives*. Different levels of managers have different responsibilities, and it is left to executive managers to select the objectives which the lower levels of management are called upon to meet. The decisions made in selecting objectives and organizing corporate resources to meet them are important tasks of planning. In fact, planning is decision making aimed at providing guidance for future operations and handling future events.

Before describing the approach to strategic planning that is the topic of this book, it is helpful to examine some of the concepts of decision making. A decision requires information and decision criteria. A pragmatic definition is:

DECISION   = INFORMATION + DECISION CRITERIA
                            (Judgment and analysis)

where

INFORMATION = DATA + INTERPRETATION
                          (Judgment and analysis)

and

JUDGMENT   = EXPERIENCE + KNOWLEDGE.

Also,

EXPERIENCE   = PREVIOUS PROBLEMS
                     + PREVIOUS ACTIONS
                     + PREVIOUS RESULTS.

The decision criteria are factors that must be considered before the most appropriate decision is reached. Some of these criteria can be quantified, others can be described concisely in words, others are expressed through standard analytical techniques such as the application of accounting ratios to a statement of accounts; but some are always judgmental. Judgment is a highly personal attribute representing the accumulated knowledge and experience of a person. Experience comes from a review of past problems, of actions taken to resolve the problems, and of the perceived results of the actions. Judgment does not enter the decision-making process only through the decision criteria. It also enters through the available information, since this is the result of interpreting available data, and the interpretation process includes judgment and standard analytical techniques.

The emphasis on the personal, subjective nature of decision making is important because that allows personal needs and feelings to be included in the strategic-planning process, and because it provides the mechanism by which two people, presented with similar information and similar formalized decision criteria, can reach different decisions, both of which may be valid. Without this, there would be only limited opportunity for creativity in planning or for distinguishing one company's strategy from another's. Other human elements, such as different sets of personal objectives, also play a major role in distinguishing plans and companies.

For complex problems (and running a business certainly falls into that class), we may not have sufficient data, validated analytical techniques, or experience to make the decisions with sufficient confidence to feel comfortable. This is another area in which the human element provides opportunities for establishing differences between companies and strategies. One owner/CEO may feel comfortable making decisions on the basis of available material while another may feel insecure because of the absence of some special information.

There is a generalized approach to handling complex problems that includes steps to develop the missing information and analytical techniques. In the process, it is usually possible to develop more experience. Figure 2-1 presents this general approach in schematic form. The first phase is an attempt to develop a better definition of the problem; the second to collect necessary data and establish formal analytical techniques that apply to the situation; and the third is decision making, involving the development of decision criteria and their application to the results of the research phase.

This process was refined during the great push by the U.S. Department of Defense to develop major weapons systems in the 1950s. Many of the complex problems addressed during that era were highly technical, involving major engineering effort. The techniques could be readily quantified, models could be developed, and decision criteria quantified. Therefore, problem definition frequently became an engineering operating analysis of the system, using highly sophisticated computer models. Good practice

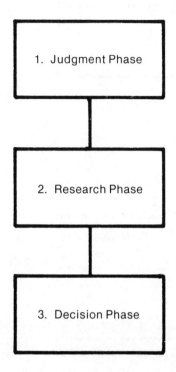

Figure 2-1. General Approach to Resolving Complex Problems

recommended that the decision criteria be quantifiable, measurable with good repeatability, unambiguous, and significant factors.

Modern management theorists would like to develop similar highly quantified techniques for decision making and strategic planning. In some instances, such as capital budgeting, they have been quite successful. It is unlikely that small businesses will have the resources to try such rigorous analysis. Therefore, we have to distill the best information from this body of experience in resolving complex problems and adapt it to the small-business situation.

The Strategic-Planning Process

Figure 2-2 shows the recommended strategic-planning process graphically. Each of the steps will be discussed individually in subsequent chapters. The

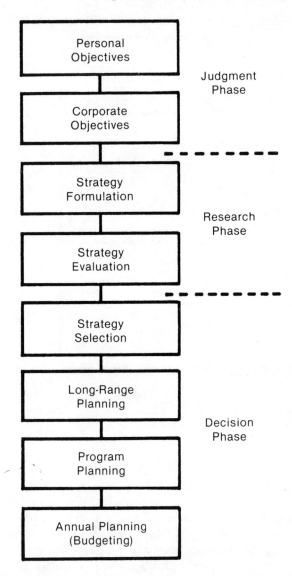

Figure 2-2. The Strategic-Planning Process for Smaller Businesses

first two steps—determining the owner/CEO's objectives and the corporate objectives—form the judgment or problem-definition phase shown in figure 2-1. The strategy-formulation and evaluation steps of figure 2-2 constitute the research phase of figure 2-1; and the final four steps of figure 2-2 are the decision phase of figure 2-1. However, there are some differences in philosophy that are not necessarily obvious from the figures. In the strategic-planning process, the decision criteria for selecting an appropriate strategy are developed during the judgment phases, not during the research or decision-making phases. There are several reasons for this. Determination of decision criteria that properly represent the wishes and intent of the owner/CEO is legitimately part of the problem-definition phase. Also, though quantifiable decision criteria are definitely best, they are not always available because of the human element in the process, and therefore it seems best to determine decision criteria during the step that involves so much personal attention. Next, this method provides for a better distribution of the work. The decision criteria are essential to reaching the best result and should not be left to lower managers or junior staff to develop. Rather, they might do the research, develop the data, and do the analyses applying the decision criteria, relieving the owner/CEO of the burden but ensuring that the important factors are properly controlled. Closely related to this separation of effort is the fact that owner/CEOs may not wish to reveal to employees their personal objectives, and may even be reluctant to reveal longer-term corporate objectives. Just exactly what is revealed to employees as a result of the strategic-planning process can be tricky, but revealing decision criteria rather than objectives is a viable compromise.

The decision phase of figure 2-1 is expanded in figure 2-2 to provide better insight into the relation between the outputs of the strategy-development process and the planning procedures that many companies already use. Both figures represent the processes as linear, with a beginning and an end. This is not always true. It is frequently necessary to repeat steps in the process and occasionally necessary to go back to the beginning to expand on the work done then. Strategic planning should be an ongoing process. There is no way to make meaningful time estimates for the durations of the steps. Also, the time horizons, that is, the period over which the work done will have validity, vary for each of the steps. The statements of objectives should only need minor changes over several years, but the plans developed to implement the chosen strategy have limited lives. The time horizon of the long-range plan depends to a large extent on the nature of the business, and the lengths of the program plans depend on the complexity of the individual programs, while the annual plans only exist for fifteen months or so (because they must be prepared in advance of the year they apply to and should be reviewed after the results are in at the end of the year in question).

There is another difference between the techniques used for resolving complex engineering problems and the techniques used for developing strategic plans. It is a well-established practice in engineering to develop mathematical models and physical models, breadboards and prototypes, of the system under examination. The mathematical models can be used to predict performance and to simulate operation of a system under a range of conditions that would be expensive or dangerous to do in practice—to investigate the impact of faults in a nuclear power plant, for example. Usually, however, the final confirmation that the correct decisions were made is the performance of a physical model. Many companies insist on a number of physical models, each fabricated at different times during the development process, to test their engineering decisions. Unfortunately, there is no equivalent to physical models in the development of strategic plans. Mathematical models have some validity in certain aspects of strategic planning, but the only physical model that can be used to test the plan is the business itself.

One feature that engineering and strategic planning share in the handling of complex problems is the ambiguity present at the beginning of the process. It is usual to find that problems, objectives, and decision criteria are ambiguously stated at first. This is a direct result of the complexity of the issues under study and is not a reflection on the capabilities of the people involved. Because this happens so frequently, it is necessary to provide for review and repetition of important tasks as ambiguities are identified and resolved. Some ambiguities can remain in the system for many years before they eventually cause problems. This is another reason why engineering groups use physical models, since their evaluation quickly reveals areas where ambiguities creep in, such as conflicting requirements in specifications.

Setting Objectives

The first and probably most important step in the whole strategic-planning process is for the owner/CEO to do a detailed self-appraisal leading to a definition of personal needs, personal objectives, and risk characteristics.

Personal needs include basics like shelter and food, and more advanced concepts like self-fulfillment. Examples of personal needs appropriate for satisfaction through a small business are status in the community, the ability to retire early, or financial security for the family. The latter need can obviously be satisfied by accumulating large sums of money, by becoming rich. Becoming rich is a direction to take in order to satisfy the personal need for financial security; owning a restaurant is an approach to becoming rich; and increasing one's net worth by $1 million over the next five years as a result of owning the restaurant is a personal objective (other writers call an objective a goal or a target). An important characteristic of an objective is that it is capable of clear definition although it need not be quantified. The intent of this example is to distinguish subjective personal needs from the directions and approaches that may be taken to satisfy those needs, and to indicate how the approach can be given concrete form by stating a suitable objective to be achieved by implementing the approach.

Clearly, there are many directions that can be taken to satisfy any particular need and many approaches to implement any particular direction. The concept of strategic logic developed by Dan R.E. Thomas of Stanford University provides a mechanism for selecting directions and approaches. Strategic logic is a set of decision criteria to select the businesses a company will operate and the allocation of resources to them. This concept was developed for use in the evaluation of strategies for major corporations but we can use it with very few modifications. Though smaller businesses usually have only one major line of business, strategic logic is still applicable. Examples are easily given. The great majority of people have definite views on whether or not to operate a legal or illegal business or a moral or immoral business. These views are based on strategic logic. Other examples are "I will go into the family business," or "Father always advised me not to go into the family business."

Strategic logic also covers the application of resources to the chosen business. Even though the common experience of small-business people is that the business demands all of their time and more, there are others who say, "I have some money to invest in a business that I wish someone else to manage." An obvious example of this is owning real estate. Others are prepared to invest everything they have in their business venture. These factors become part of the strategic logic of the owner/CEOs.

Identifying needs, personal objectives, and the appropriate strategic logic require self-appraisal by the owner/CEO. This is true whether referring to a new venture or an existing business. Self-appraisal is a very difficult process, since individuals are usually the last to know their biases, strengths, and weaknesses, even though those around them have known these things for years. Yet self-appraisal is essential to start the strategic-planning process.

During the self-appraisal, we must come to terms with risk. The dictionary defines *risk* as "A chance of encountering harm or loss."[1] Strictly speaking, a business faces uncertainty rather than risk since it is always possible that the peformance of the business may be better than anticipated. The term risk is preferred here because the emotional connotation of the word has value, reminding us of the need to perform strategic planning to maintain the business in a state of readiness to respond to changes in the environment. Because the owner/CEO of a small business usually has great longevity with the business, maintaining the self-appraisal current is important.

Setting corporate objectives means relating them to the individual needs identified in the self-appraisal. If the most important need is to establish an estate to be willed to the children, then a reasonable corporate objective would be long-term growth in the owner's equity. However, the objectives must be tempered by the business's ability to satisfy them. A professional business such as a small consulting firm is not likely to provide significant growth in equity. Therefore, it is essential to be as objective as possible in performing the self-appraisal, setting personal objectives, establishing the strategic logic, and establishing corporate objectives. Arbitrary statements like "my strategic logic is to run a five-star hotel" must be critically reviewed. For one thing, the statement sounds more like an approach than strategic logic. But what is to happen in this case if current resources are only enough to operate a campground? A better statement of strategic logic would be "my business will be in the travel industry," but even this needs more refinement before it becomes part of an applicable strategic logic.

The final task of setting objectives is to reconcile the personal objectives, strategic logic, and corporate objectives to minimize the chance of amgiguities, and to consolidate the progress made for the next step.

Strategy Formulation, Evaluation, and Selection

Objectives of Strategies

The next major step in the strategy-planning process is to develop several strategies that, if implemented, could help the company achieve its objectives. This requires an evaluation of the company's current status, and a comparison of that with the desired status. In this way, it is possible to develop a picture of the areas of corporate strength and weakness, and to determine how the company's performance falls short of that desired. The first objective of the strategies is to provide guidance for modifying the business operations in order to reposition the company and make it more likely that the corporate objectives will be achieved. The second objective is to map out how the company will actually achieve the desired objectives.

Basic Strategic Options

There are several strategies that occur frequently among both large and small companies. They can be referred to as *natural strategies*. In the brief discussion given here, both products and services are called products. One way to classify these natural strategies is by the way in which companies respond to markets, especially to changes in markets. Table 2-1 shows the four major natural market-response strategies and their major characteristics. Some small businesses, especially those with entrepreneurial characteristics, follow strategy *a*; hardly any small businesses follow strategy *b*, at least for an extended time; most small businesses are in class *c* (the late-to-market strategy); and some are in class *d*. This distribution is not necessarily the optimum for any industry or for any individual small company.

Table 2-1
Natural Market-Response Strategies

Strategy	Characteristics
First to market	Requires state-of-the-art knowledge, ability to stimulate primary demand, good timing, and access to capital.
Second to market	Requires flexibility, speed of response, and ability to differentiate products.
Late to market	Requires low product costs, low overhead, and efficiency of operations.
Market segmentation	Requires good awareness of customer needs, product specialization, some flexibility, and concentration of resources.

A second important classification is by scale. Table 2-2 shows the two major natural strategies for large-scale businesses, obviously an area in which by definition small businesses have difficulties competing; and the market-segmentation (niche) strategy appropriate for smaller businesses.

A third classification of natural strategies is by major operating characteristics of the company. Many owner/CEOs view their businesses as fitting into one of the classes shown in table 2-3.

Obviously, the different classifications of natural strategies overlap. In practice, those listed here represent major strategies followed by a large number of businesses. There is actually a range of possibilities including many combinations of the major discrete strategies and many other more specialized strategies. It is this range that provides the opportunity for

Table 2-2
Natural Scale Strategies

Strategy	Characteristics
Low cost	Large-scale, industry leader, high-efficiency production and distribution, probably standardized or commodity products, and tight cost control
Market-share maximization	Requires product differentiation; customers must perceive product uniqueness either through technology, brand name, or product features; control over product technology; and ability to insert large barriers to competitor's entry such as major capital investments.
Market segmentation	Requires good awareness of customer needs, product specialization, some flexibility, and concentration of resources.

Table 2-3
Natural Operating Strategies

Strategy	Characteristics
Entrepreneurial	Risk-taking, growth-oriented, often innovative.
Product-oriented	Largely introspective, sell what is made, product ideas from staff or competitors.
Market-dedicated	Largely customer-oriented, often with geographical limitations, often without product-development or manufacturing facilities.
Value added in manufacturing	Related to product-oriented, usually small-volume high-margin, or high-volume low-margin products.
Value added in marketing	Related to market-dedicated, usually high-volume or high-value products.

forming custom strategies appropriate to the circumstances of individual companies, and the mechanism for satisfying the broad range of corporate objectives related to the different needs of owner/CEOs. It also provides the vehicle for the personality and experience of the planner to influence the strategy, distinguishing it from that of competitors.

Strategy Formulation

Strategy formulation can take place at several levels of sophistication. The basic level is to select a strategy from the natural strategies that has the best match with the company's strengths and the best chance of achieving the corporate objectives. The next level is to formulate a strategy that exploits company strengths, satisfies corporate objectives, and positions the company to take advantage of competitors' weaknesses. The highest level of sophistication considered here is the formulation of a strategy that achieves objectives by exploiting company strengths and competitors' weaknesses through modifications to the industry/market environment that emphasize a company's own strengths and the others' weaknesses. The strategy may also be used to blunt competitors' strengths and mask the company's own weaknesses. The different levels of strategy can also be viewed as one-dimensional, two-dimensional, and three-dimensional representations of the planned response to the same set of circumstances.

The Danger of Strategy Forming by Default

All businesses have a strategy but for many it is formed by default. There is a tendency to think that alternative approaches are not relevant because "We have always done things this way." This justification avoids facing uncomfortable or threatening issues or decisions. It also endows predecessors with an almost magical ability to determine and implement the best way to operate the business, and it ignores the fact that the environments in which the business operates are always changing, as well as the fact that the business itself is changing. Strengths are not recognized and exploited, and weaknesses are not identified and eradicated. Another reason that strategies form by default is poor communication within a company. When this occurs, employees make pragmatic short-term decisions that cumulatively form an ad-hoc strategy. Usually, these decisions are made in good faith on the assumption that they represent the owner/CEO's wishes and objectives. Occasionally, they are made to serve the interest of the decision maker interested in self-advancement or in righting some personal grievance. In any case, strategy formed by default almost never meets suitable corporate and personal objectives, nor prepares the business for long-term survival in the face of changing conditions.

Analytical Evaluation Techniques

We have said that making decisions requires information, analysis, and decision criteria. Techniques of analysis are characterized by formality and are most often quantitative. Once the technique has been described and taught to analysts, it should be capable of uniform application so that each analyst comes to at least similar, if not identical, conclusions when provided with the same data and information. A major advantage is that analysis can be delegated to others, relieving the owner/CEO of the burden and freeing scarce executive time. Other advantages of such analysis are: quantitative results are usually unambiguous if the correct analytical approach is selected; it is possible to test for accuracy and reproducibility of the results; it is possible to ask "what if . . . ?" questions expanding the range of the analysis (in particular, sensitivity analyses can be performed showing how the outcome of several possible decisions changes as significant factors are changed); and the results are readily recorded. Unfortunately, analytical techniques have several problems. Many factors cannot be quantified, although sophisticated techniques exist for the attempt to do so. Therefore, many analyses must use extensive sets of assumptions, and many desirable analyses are not possible at all. Other problems include the facts that numerical results are frequently invested with significance and authority not justified by the analysis; though they may be reproducible and precise, they may not be relevant or accurate in the sense of representing the true situation (great precision and little accuracy is common in many analyses such as market projections and overhead calculations); and the significance of quantitative results is not easily communicated, since they are capable of interpretation. Nevertheless, formal analytical techniques should be used where possible, bearing in mind that they must be modified by using judgment and that they must not dominate the decision-making process just because they are quantitative.

Strategy Selection

The strategy-formulation and evaluation processes should produce a rank-ordered list of possible strategies. Usually, one major strategy survives the planning process as others are discredited and dropped during evaluation, and this strategy often has several options and alternatives associated with it. It would be quite remarkable for two distinct, viable strategies to emerge from the process. It is imperative not to assume that the surviving strategy is automatically the right strategy to pursue. If the planning process has been implemented diligently, the best strategy should be better than the existing and presumably ad-hoc strategy, but it may not be good enough to achieve the corporate objectives. So time should be taken to review critically the best strategy and its main alternatives before acceptance. It is essential to feel comfortable with the selected strategy, and this additional time is always well spent. It does not need to be an intensive study unless some critical issue is identified. A good analogy is the recommendation made by teachers of writing to lay a draft text aside for a couple of days between revisions so that you return to it with a fresh mind and some enhanced level of objectivity. However, there are some practical constraints. If it is already clear that the current strategy is an ad hoc one, then the new strategy should offer some advantages. Also, the business may be facing some testing situations—new competitors in the local market, obsolete products, or an extended recession for example—that require a response. Pressure is an excellent incentive in human activities.

Once a strategy is selected, the emphasis turns to preparing the plans necessary to convert the concepts developed into guidance for the day-to-day operations of the business. However, the selection process should not be forgotten. There will be ambiguities in the original statement of the strategies that must be resolved. Many of these can be resolved by referring back to the evaluation and selection processes. Some may need expansion of some part of the strategy plan, including new data collection, analysis, and evaluation. Also, as time passes, the decision criteria used during the original selection process become dated and new ones are needed. Strategies designed to consolidate the company's balance sheet may be needed before loans are solicited for the construction of a new factory while strategies designed to improve cash flow will be needed during the subsequent expansion in operations. Another example with more far-reaching consequences is the transfer of a family business from one generation to the next, especially when the transfer is triggered by a death or when the younger owner/CEO has just married.

Planning

Plans are the end products of the strategy-planning process. They are the vehicle used to communicate the strategy to employees who must implement it, they are the tools to implement strategy, and the maps and mileposts by which progress is measured. For most small businesses only three main classes of plans are necessary. More tend to confuse the organization and certainly to tie up valuable executive time unnecessarily. The three classes are the long-range plan, the program plans, and the annual plan, commonly called the budget. The long-range plan translates the strategy plan into operating objectives, decision-making guidance for operating decisions, and programs to implement the strategy. The time horizon of the long-range plan varies from business to business. A manufacturer of equipment used in military systems or major capital products like electrical-power generating stations can adopt a time horizon of several years, probably five to seven, with confidence that it is meaningful. On the other hand, a distributor of electronic components or a store selling personal computers should adopt a shorter time horizon, two to three years, because of the rapidly changing nature of the industries they operate in.

The program plans are detailed statements of the individual tasks required to implement the strategy. Each must include detailed objectives for the program, its relation to other programs, its significance in the strategy, the resources needed for successful implementation, review and success criteria for monitoring progress, names of responsible people, and schedules. A program may have a time horizon stretching from a few weeks to the time horizon of the long-range plan. The annual plan or annual budget is usually a financial document with objectives for the year stated quantitatively. It must accommodate all the essential programs operating during that year including those that start, stop, or just operate throughout the year. It is also important for guiding and monitoring day-to-day operations.

Other commonly used types of plans are capital plans, product plans, personnel plans, and so on. In this framework, these are treated as components of one of the major classes of plans discussed here. For most small businesses, the capital plan becomes part of the annual plan with longer-term considerations included in the long-range plan. Some smaller businesses may need a separate long-range capital plan but even so, this is usually a by-product of the long-range plan rather than a stand-alone document created separately for the purpose. Product plans, personnel plans, and so on are treated as program plans even though they continue in one form or another for many years. In this way, the owner/CEO is forced to review all the activities of the company at regular intervals rather than allowing them to continue without critical review. This can be particularly important for products that tend to stay in production as long as there are orders even if they are no longer profitable, because they require a high level of warranty support for example.

Discussion

What are we trying to achieve during the strategic-planning process? We are seeking information and insights to establish meaningful objectives, possible approaches to reach the objectives, decision criteria to select the best approach, and plans to implement the selected approach. A systematic strategic-planning approach is recommended so that the planner considers all the issues that experience has shown to be important in an ordered manner that eases their coordination into the final plan.

Note

1. Funk & Wagnalls Standard Desk Dictionary (New York: Funk & Wagnalls, Inc., 1974), p. 576.

3 Setting Objectives

"Our plans miscarry because they have no aim. When a man does not know what harbor he is making for, no wind is the right wind." —Seneca

This chapter covers the tricky problem of developing personal and corporate objectives that are compatible and realistic. The topical coverage of this chapter and its relation to the rest of the planning process is indicated in figure 3-1. These steps require detailed consideration of personal and interpersonal issues and their relationship to the business. The main issues considered are personal needs, personal attitude toward risk, strategic logic, and the other parties (actors) involved. We do not need to be experts in psychology, statistics, or game theory to gain valuable insights about what we do and why we do it, or to learn how to identify strengths, weaknesses, and biases by discussing some of the findings of these sciences. By doing so we can open a wider range of possibilities and develop ways to evaluate and select among them. The possibilities occur at every level from business problems to individual problems.

Needs and Objectives

As indicated in chapter 2, needs and objectives are closely related. Needs are highly subjective; basically everyone has the same set of needs although the emphasis placed on each need by different individuals varies widely. Objectives are concrete expressions of particular needs that the individual wishes to satisfy, in this case through the operation of a small business. The intent of this discussion is to increase awareness of the relationship between business activities and personal needs, to indicate some of the many alternative objectives that could conceivably satisfy specific needs, and to provide insight into ways of selecting acceptable alternatives. The emphasis is not on describing in detail the various combinations of human needs but on the fact that everyone has a personal combination of needs that must be recognized, at least in broad outline, for use in later steps in the strategic-planning process in order to increase the chances that operating a business will produce personal satisfaction.

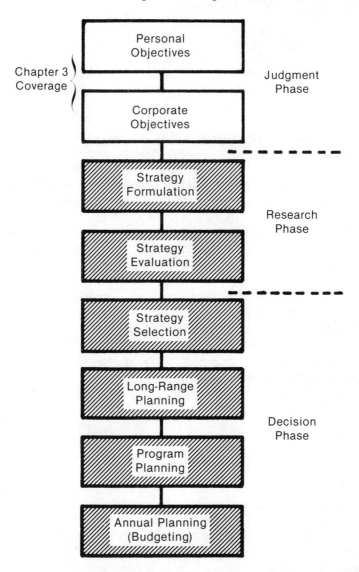

Figure 3-1. The Strategic-Planning Process for Smaller Businesses (Chapter 3 Coverage)

Background

The study of human needs is part of the broad and expanding fields of psychiatry, psychology, and sociology. Businesspeople usually refer to needs only when discussing ways in which employees can be motivated to perform more work, or to produce higher quality products. Even in this limited area there is an extensive body of knowledge and many theories. The basic assumption is that if a manager can identify what an employee's needs are, then a personal contract can be established in which the employee's needs are satisfied in return for the desired work output. An excellent summary of the theories of motivation is contained in an article by David Terpstra.[1]

The study of needs is complex because each employee has individualized needs that change with time. Furthermore, individuals respond to the satisfaction of needs in different ways. Herzberg and collaborators proposed that for some needs the opposite of *satisfaction* is not *dissatisfaction* but rather *no satisfaction*. Similarly, steps taken to alleviate dissatisfaction do not produce an opposite state of satisfaction but a state of *no dissatisfaction*. The owner/CEO struggling to develop personal objectives as the starting point for a strategic plan should not worry about resolving apparent paradoxes like this, but he should recognize that identifying the most important personal needs to satisfy through the business will take time.

Abraham Maslow established a starting point for considering human needs more than forty years ago. He proposed the since well-known hierarchy of needs starting with basic physiological needs such as food and shelter (level one), moving to the need for long-term security in the supply of food and shelter (level two), then to need to belong to a social group (level three), and then the higher needs of self-esteem and achievement (levels four and five). According to Terpstra, there is little evidence that people are motivated by an opportunity to move to a higher level in this hierarchy, presumably because most people in a business environment already have addressed, although not necessarily satisfied, all levels of needs. Owner/CEOs will usually be most interested in determining their needs in levels three, four, and five (social needs, self-esteem, and achievement), although ensuring continued security (level two) can be very important. Individuals with a strong need to satisfy level-three social needs ought to be especially careful in selecting objectives; they must remember the Herzberg paradoxes when examining the possible impact of their decisions on others and their wish, perhaps, to motivate others to help reach their objectives (see also the comments to follow on actors affected by the planning process).

Herzberg proposed that motivating workers requires attention to ten factors divided into two groups of five. The first group, called the hygiene factors, contains in order of importance salary, growth possibilities, relations with subordinates, status, and relations with superiors. According to Herzberg, attention to hygiene factors does not improve motivation nor increase satisfaction, it only produces no dissatisfaction. The second group of factors, which can be used for motivational purposes and to produce satisfaction, contains in order of importance achievement, recognition, the job itself, responsibility, and advancement. Terpstra suggests that the theory is flawed but admits that it provides valuable insights into human behavior. Others believe that the ten factors are not in the correct order, and there have been several challenges to the concept that hygiene factors cannot produce satisfaction.

There is general agreement that establishing challenging objectives is an important factor in motivating human behavior and satisfying needs. Of course, imposing challenging objectives on others does not guarantee success, but the owner/CEO should recognize the benefits that come from setting such objectives for himself. The disadvantage is that later recognition of an objective as unachievable can also be a powerful negative factor. The expectancy/valence theory of motivation includes three factors: the recognition that increased efforts to achieve an objective will improve performance; the recognition that improved performance will increase the chances of rewards; and the value placed on the rewards by the individual. Although the theories discussed here were developed to describe ways that can be used by one person to motivate others, they contain principles that apply to the identification of personal needs and the objectives to meet in order to satisfy them.

Developing Personal Objectives

The complexity of personal needs and motivation demands that the owner/CEO develop a careful list of specific objectives that are related to identified important needs. The list should be short: one item is acceptable although most people will include two or three, related to different aspects of their needs. In chapter 2 the example was given of satisfying the need for security by operating a restaurant in such a way that personal net worth would be increased significantly over a period of time. A second objective, aimed at satisfying self-esteem and achievement needs, could be to gain recognition as a gourmet restaurant by listings in exclusive guides or extensive media coverage in appropriate magazines. A third objective, related to satisfying social needs, could be retention of the business in the family on retirement.

Restricting the list of personal objectives has the following advantages:

eliminating objectives that appear attractive but extend the list focuses attention on the details of the process;

having too many objectives leads to diffusion of effort, which may endanger the achievement of any of them;

having too many objectives increases the chances of conflicts among them; and the elimination process highlights some of the possible conflicts that exist at an early stage.

Quantifying objectives where possible also helps the owner/CEO later. The easiest objectives to quantify are the financial and time objectives. Quantitative objectives are simply communicated and easily monitored. However, they should not be allowed to dominate the setting of objectives because of this. It is impossible to forecast events with accuracy. The restaurant example shows how a quantitative objective can be deceptive. Achieving a net worth of $1 million is meaningless if in the intervening period inflation erodes the value of the dollar significantly or if the book value of the real estate forms a large proportion of the net-worth figure and other changes in the area have reduced its realizable value. Numerical analysis is only a guide. Numbers are not objectives but measures of objectives.

Personal Attitudes toward Risk

One important theme of this book is to encouarge the strategic planner to adopt an objective approach to the strategic-planning process; that is, not to let emotions or personal biases unreasonably limit the alternatives investigated. However, objectivity does not mean that every issue or every decision has to be reduced to quantitative terms and the plan with the best quantitative analysis followed. There are three problems with the quantitative approach:

1. Not every issue can be quantified. How do you place a dollar value on the quality of life?
2. The calculations will involve other assumptions that will affect the quantitative answers. How can a happily married owner/CEO include the impact of a divorce that is not anticipated?
3. People respond differently to decisions even when numbers are provided. Their response depends on their attitude toward risk.

This section is intended to increase awareness of the subjective nature of attitudes toward risk, so that the owner/CEO can adopt a more detached position in the selection of personal and corporate objectives. A better understanding of risk also helps in detailed strategic planning when it is necessary to accommodate possible actions by competitors in the process. Individual attitudes toward risk differ just as individual needs differ, and an understanding of the differences also helps the planning process.

Studies of risk have been undertaken by psychiatrists, psychologists, financial institutions, military planners, and business planners. Many books and articles have been published on the subject but a recent article by Kahneman and Tversky provides excellent insights.[2] A simple way to check the statement that people have different views of risk is to ask a question like this: "You have a choice between a gift to you of some amount of money, X, and a free lottery ticket with which you have a 90-percent chance of winning $100 or a 10-percent chance of winning $0. For what size gift is the choice unimportant to you?" Strict mathematical analysis shows that the value of the lottery ticket to the chooser is $90 ($100 × 90% + $0 × 10%). However, most people will select a value for the gift less than $90; answers in the $60-to-$80 range are not unusual. There is a definite tendency to try to avoid the risk that they will not gain anything at all, even though it is only one chance in ten.

The situation concerning the avoidance of losses is different. Most people will accept the risk of a large loss in order to have a small chance of avoiding a certain loss. The question to elucidate this type of information is the reverse of the earlier one: "You have a choice between a definite loss to you of Y, and a situation in which you have a 90-percent chance of losing $100 or a 10-percent chance of losing $0. At what value of Y is the choice unimportant to you?" Most people will again respond in the range of $60 to $80 although there is some evidence that the same person will give a slightly higher number in the loss case than in the gain case. In the loss case, the individual is hoping to benefit from the 10-percent chance of losing nothing and has actually sought out the risk in the hope of avoiding the loss.

What else can be learned from a review of existing decision theory that can help in detailed self-appraisal of personal risk tendencies? The scale of the decision and the anticipated impact of possible outcomes plays an important role. Generally, people seek to avoid risk in selecting between gains and to accept risk in selecting between losses. However, for very low probabilities of a large gain or a large loss, the typical response is to inflate the probabilities and this can lead to a situation in which risk is sought out rather than avoided in selecting between two opportunities for gain; or risk is avoided rather than sought out in selecting between two sources of loss. The standard example of this is the decision to buy a state lottery ticket when the price is $1, the prize $250,000, and the chances of winning are one in a million. The mathematical value of the lottery ticket is only $0.25, but people either do not know or do not evaluate the meaning of the winning odds of one in a million. The spoilsport reminds them that the chances of losing $1 are 999,999 in 1,000,000. At the other extreme, even very small chances of losing so much money that one's lifestyle would be changed drastically are avoided.

There are other ways in which strict adherence to numbers is modified by personal attitudes toward risk. The common perception is that the difference between gains of $100 and $200 is much more important than the difference between gains of $1,000 and $1,100. The same bias is observed when discussing losses. Obviously people look at the ratio rather than the absolute amount when making their subjective decisions.

Emotional responses to risk can play a role also. People asked to choose between alternatives to combat some catastrophe will change their choices depending on the way the information is presented. Assume there has been an earthquake in some remote location and five hundred people will die unless they receive aid very quickly. Unfortunately, the rescuers have to choose between two alternative aid programs: one program will save two hundred people while the other has a 40-percent chance of saving everybody and 60-percent chance that no one will be saved. Most people will select the approach that avoids the risk and choose the first program to save two hundred people. If the same situation is presented to another group of people in a different way, the favored choice changes. The first program means that three hundred people will die while the second program means that there is a 60-percent chance that everyone will die and a 40-percent chance that no one will die. Now, people perceive the choice as one between the certain death of three hundred people and a small chance that no one will die. They prefer to take the risk in choosing between losses.

This response is called a *framing effect* by behavioral psychiatrists. The individual makes decisions with reference to some point, and, if the point is changed, the decision can be changed. In the earthquake example, the first group tended to refer to the death of five hundred people and judge the alternatives as gains (lives saved) while the second group tended to refer to zero deaths and select between programs on the basis of lives lost. Frequently, the reference point is only imagined: which is worse, the loss of $50 in cash or the loss of a new $50 calculator? There are no correct answers to questions like this.

Naturally, people can only make judgments based on their own experience, and to the extent that personal experience filters out certain information, the judgments are biased. Every airliner crash is reported in detail by the news media but the great majority of car crashes are ignored except for a few lines in the local newspaper. This promotes the feeling that air travel is more risky than it is and car travel less risky. This limitation in experience contributes to *framing*, *anchoring*, and *adjustment* (to be discussed), and the use of imagination in the absence of other information.

Another pertinent psychological phenomenon is called *discounting*. Possible major events that are remote in time or distance are not as important as minor local activities that are close by and imminent. This also colors the development of estimates of the risk involved in certain objectives.

An exception to discounting that is frequently met is attitudes toward possible catastrophes. Any event that would have catastrophic consequences, whose occurrence is not under the control of the observer, and that is not fully understood, no matter how unlikely it is to occur, is subject to the reverse of discounting, a great apprehension that the catastrophe is virtually assured of happening. Fortunately, this class of event is more a political problem affecting things such as public policy toward nuclear power plants, for example, than a small-business problem.

The message here is to alert the strategic planner to the existence of inherent tendencies in everyone to modify the meanings of numbers when it comes to evaluating risks. Even when alerted to this, many find it difficult to adjust their first estimate of the risk after they have made their first judgment; this is called *anchoring* and *adjustment*.[3]

Risk, Uncertainty, and Ignorance

Decision makers usually try to distinguish among risk, uncertainty, and ignorance. A situation is said to involve risk if all possible outcomes and the probabilities with which they may occur are known. A situation is said to involve uncertainty if the probabilities that some of the outcomes will occur are not known. Ignorance implies that not all the possible outcomes are known. In principle, it should be possible to turn a situation in which ignorance prevails into at least one involving only uncertainty, and a situation involving uncertainty into one involving only risk.

However, developing information to make these changes involves time, effort, and money, so one has to decide whether obtaining the extra information is worth the effort and expense. In strictly quantitative situations, it is usually possible to calculate how much expense is justified to improve knowledge about possible outcomes. Returning to the rhetorical question of whether one would choose a 90-percent chance of losing $100 or a 10-percent chance of losing $0, if the random loss has already been determined but the information is not yet published, how much is it worth to the chooser to buy that information before making the decision between the random loss and the certain loss? Clearly not more than the $60-to-$80 loss most people were contemplating. So even perfect information has a limited value.

Measuring Risk

Decision theory in regard to risk and uncertainty makes frequent reference to probabilities, distributions, and other terms associated with statistics and probability theory. These are accepted measures of risk. Statistics can be very helpful in certain situations. They allow us to present a precise numerical description of a group of objects, people, or events. They are developed by making measurements of a large number of people or objects. If the subject is an event, statistics are accumulated from many measurements of repetitions of the event.

Statistics might seem to offer little help to the small-business person dealing with discrete events such as the setting of objectives in the presence of great uncertainty. He needs to predict the outcome of certain events that only occur once or a limited number of times. Fortunately, statistics do provide guidance in making these predictions. If sufficient data are available, many possible outcomes can be eliminated from consideration because they occur infrequently. The data should help determine which are the most likely occurrences, although it might be very difficult to distinguish among several outcomes that have nearly equal frequencies of occurrence. Recently, advanced techniques have been developed to assign probabilities to occurrences.[4] However, for our purposes it is sufficient to remember that probability estimates of the occurrence of one event are more a measure of the maker's confidence in his prediction than a prediction of outcome. As new information becomes available, the predictor usually modifies the probabilities even though the event itself has not changed any of its characteristics.

Practical Decision Making

Another feature that distinguishes the objective description of risk using statistics from the individual decisions that an owner/CEO must make is the intervention of the owner/CEO in the decision-making process. A situation may involve risk in the strict sense that all the possible outcomes and their frequencies of occurrence are known, but the decision maker has to decide which occurrence will be next. In fact, the first risk to be confronted is whether to participate or make a decision at all. Once that decision is made, the selection of one possibility rather than another is a one-time choice that can be guided by probability information and modified by the risk-taking attitudes of the decision maker.

Everyone in business has to be prepared to face the risks of doing business, but not everyone is the stereotypical entrepreneur who is apparently prepared to take larger risks than most in order to gain a larger-than-usual return. The issue is not one of reckless risk taking without caution or fear of loss, but the distinction between the nature of the "game" each individual is prepared to participate in. In the game analogy, some might prefer poker, in which the loss of only one hand is risked and the game continues, while others might prefer checkers or chess, in which risks can be avoided or at least hedged but one mistake usually ends the game.

The thoughtful businessperson also categorizes risks as avoidable or unavoidable, and as acceptable or unacceptable. Clearly, avoidable risks should not be contemplated unless they are very precisely defined and their consequences controllable if necessary. Unacceptable risks should also be shunned. Some are prepared to trade increased risk against hoped-for increased return, using their willingness to make personal sacrifice as a buffer if things go wrong. It is in this area that the need to discuss personal objectives with the other actors (see the next section) becomes critical. Nevertheless, every owner/CEO recognizes the need to make sacrifices in the interests of the business, and to take clearly identified, monitorable risks when they are unavoidable, even if part of the personal sacrifice is erosion of peace of mind.

The Actors

The next step in developing explicit personal objectives to be pursued through the operations of a small business is to review the actors—individuals and organizations—who will be affected by them. The business will affect many others with their own (frequently conflicting) objectives, objectives usually not revealed to the owner/CEO and often unclear even to the person or organization pursuing them. A further complexity is that the population of actors and their objectives are continually changing. It is not worthwhile to attempt to identify every possible combination of actors and objectives that affect an individual, so part of the review is to determine which must be accommodated and which can safely be ignored.

The actors fall into three main groups: individuals with whom a personal relationship exists; individuals with whom a business relationship exists; and organizations with whom a business relationship exists.

Personal Relationships

Personal relationships include family members, joint owners (investors or partners), executives and managers, employees, and professional advisors. Common failings that put stress on personal relationships are easily listed but not so easily avoided. They include:

failure to discuss personal objectives and their importance to the individuals concerned;

failure to recognize that valid differences in personal objectives can exist and that they need to be accommodated;

attempts to impose personal objectives on others, either consciously or subconsciously;

failure to identify changes in individuals, especially changes in experience, education, and maturity; and

failure to communicate expectations.

These factors cause stress in many family-operated businesses also, stress that can affect operations negatively. The informed owner/CEO tries to avoid them in the setting of personal objectives and during day-to-day business operations. Of course, the owner/CEO must retain authority over the business, so if conflicts cannot be resolved after good-faith attempts have been made to do so, the owner/CEO ought to state that continued participation in the business by a family member or other personal relation is contingent on that person accepting certain objectives, policies, and plans to achieve them. Preferably, this is only done after the owner/CEO has gone through all the stages of strategic planning including setting personal objectives, with full recognition of the actors affected, and has communicated the results to the others involved.

Other individuals whose personal wishes and preferences must be considered include partners and investors in a privately held company. It has been suggested by some who have experienced the problems of a partnership with a poor-communications problem that the relationship can be as emotionally stimulating or trying as a marriage. The same principles used in setting objectives apply to handling differences in expectations. Since major objectives are only set and modified infrequently, stress from failure to communicate expectations is common. How many hours a week are expected? What about vacations? Which comes first, the business or other activities? These are common areas of disagreement requiring a conflict-resolution mechanism to maintain harmonious relationships.

It is rare that other personal relationships have the emotional depth associated with family or ownership relationships. In these other relationships the owner/CEO feels much freer to say, "This is the way it is going to be." Yet in established businesses, the owner/CEO developing a detailed strategic plan for the first time will find that there are many unstated commitments to and from executives and senior managers. In general, most of these commitments will have little impact on setting personal objectives, or they can be readily accommodated. But they should be reviewed to determine which, if any, deserve further attention. Obvious examples are the manager about to marry into the family, or the executive with stock options, or large, unfunded accruals such as bonuses and pensions. In these cases, the owner/CEO must consider the other actor's response to changes in personal objectives and determine whether it will cause problems. Even if it does, this does not mean that the objectives should be changed, but the possible penalties should be considered before the objectives are finally adopted and communicated to others.

In many very small companies, there is also a close relationship between the owner/CEO and the staff. This can cause heartache if satisfying the personal and company objectives requires closing or selling the company or bringing in new staff to implement changes beyond the competence of the existing staff. Again, these things should be considered, not to cause unreasonable modifications in the legitimate personal objectives of the owner/CEO, but to alert him to factors that must be considered during the planning and implementation stages.

Many owner/CEOs feel isolated, with little opportunity to talk to others about their hopes and fears, let alone about specific business problems. For some, the solution is to establish a good relationship with a professional advisor, frequently an accountant or attorney, or perhaps a banker, consultant, a friend in a similar business, or a colleague in a professional organization. Some of these people can also be viewed as individuals with whom a business relationship exists. Their value increases if the relationship extends beyond the conventional business relationship to include discussion of personal issues. It is unlikely that there will be a conflict over personal objectives with a professional advisor, although tremendous pressure may be exerted to modify or at least review them. Of course, this changes if the advisor has a financial interest in the business; a common case with bankers.

Business Relationships with Individuals

Personal relationships with family members and other owners tend to provide incentives for selecting financial objectives and limits on the ways these objectives can be specified and achieved. Business relationships with individuals tend to provide inspiration for a wide-ranging review of possible objectives and a sense of reality about what is a sensible objective and what is unreasonable, at least as far as business activities are concerned. As a result, such relationships are productive during the objective-setting phase of strategic planning. Their importance derives from the independence and objectivity of those involved, so the owner/CEO should look for warning signals that might indicate a lack of objectivity when a business friend strongly promotes a particular viewpoint. As before, obvious indicators are the establishment of a financial relationship such as investor, creditor, or debtor, or a change in the personal relationship itself. For example, there would be no conflict of interest with an accountant who was paid for auditing the books and preparing tax returns and who also advised on the opportunities available to companies in the same industry, unless the accountant became a major creditor or began having problems with his own business that might be eased if the owner/CEO followed a certain course of action. Receiving a fee for specific tasks does not destroy independence and objectivity unless the fee is a major part of the recipient's livelihood. Even so, if the conflict of interest is recognized, the discussions can still be valuable. The combination of independence, objectivity, and friendship is a powerful aid to an owner/CEO seeking to establish meaningful personal objectives that feel comfortable.

Business Relationships with Organizations

In general, these are the least important of the three classes of relationships discussed here. However, there are certain circumstances in which they become very significant. Direct financial relationships with investors, creditors, and debtors need consideration. In these cases, the attitudes of the key individuals toward the owner/CEO's announced or perceived objectives can be critical. In many circumstances, assumptions are made about the owner/CEO's objectives in the absence of factual information, assumptions that lead to actions that affect the small business and perhaps the personal interests of the owner/CEO. The solution is to hold frank discussions with the key individuals in the organizations concerned, especially if a change in plans is under consideration. There are several benefits to doing this. The independence and objectivity of the other parties provides insight into what is reasonable or possible and establishes a realistic basis for personal objectives. It also helps establish a framework for later work on the strategic plan, in particular the conversion of the personal objectives to compatible business objectives (see later in this chapter). People are always flattered to be consulted on such matters—a natural human response—but they can also be impressed at the professionalism of the owner/CEO's approach to strategic planning. This favorable impression can be turned to good use later if larger investments or loans are required to implement the resulting plan or if existing loans must be extended.

Other times when business organizations become important in setting objectives occur when there are conflicts or synergies between business strategies. These can best be seen if the organizations are divided into suppliers, customers, and competitors. More complex situations with one major organization as supplier, customer, and competitor can occur but are not discussed further here. In all three cases, conflicting business strategies can occur that affect the smaller business and its reasonable hopes for achieving certain objectives. The owner/CEO may wish to set financial independence as an objective but be engaged in a business in which the strategy of a major corporate supplier is to ensure that its small customers are financially dependent so that its market can be controlled. There have been allegations that this has happened in the oil industry between oil companies and service stations, and in some franchise businesses. This is a real problem for the owner/CEO who must determine what constitutes financial independence and how important it is to achieve it. Similarly, a small business may seek growth in order to satisfy some personal objective but be engaged in supplying products and services to customers in a limited-growth or zero-growth industry. Again, the conflict between intent and reality must be resolved, probably at the stage of clarifying personal objectives but certainly at the stage of setting business objectives.

Major companies may determine that in order to be competitive in their own industries they must integrate their business operations vertically either forward or backward, possibly displacing a small business entirely or trying to acquire it, just as the owner/CEO of the small business had decided that his personal objectives included retirement in ten years. These changes are difficult to elucidate and even frank discussions with key individuals in the larger company are likely to be less than frank when it comes to details of the major company's business strategy. Many other changes in strategy by larger companies that can affect small businesses are more difficult to identify even when they are being implemented. For example, a customer may decide to control inventories of purchased materials more closely; a vendor may phase out a product or adjust prices to discourage small purchasers.

Yet all is not gloom for the small business. Changes in strategy by larger businesses can provide excellent opportunities for smaller companies. The distribution industry is varied and complex, ranging from fresh foodstuffs to capital equipment; moving through agents, manufacturer's representatives, distributors, wholesalers, retailers, warehouses, and shipping companies. Major companies may decide to change their sales-and-distribution strategy to improve their competitiveness, thus providing opportunities for small businesses. A good example is the increase in the number of retail stores selling personal computers. Many office-equipment dealers are considering whether to add computers to their product lines. In some cases this examination will have to include a review of the owner/CEO's personal objectives and risk-taking tendencies.

Finally, every business has competitors whose existence must be recognized to ensure a realistic basis for the personal objectives finally chosen.

Development of Strategic Logic

Strategic logic is the set of decision criteria used by the owner/CEO to select directions and approaches to satisfying personal objectives; in particular, which business to be in, the style of operation, and the utilization of resources. Many of those in ongoing businesses will be surprised that decision criteria are required for this purpose. Intellectually, the selection of a business, operating style, and resources are recognized as decisions to be made. Pragmatically, what choice is there? The decisions have all been made so why worry about strategic logic? The answer is that a review of the way in which the decisions were made will provide more insight into setting corporate objectives, help link them to personal objectives, and potentially reveal new opportunities. It is doubtful that major changes will come out of this review unless a new business or a major change in business activities is under consideration. However, it will also be surprising if there are not some changes as a result of this review.

Elements of Strategic Logic

Before giving some examples of strategic logic, let us examine more closely what is meant by a business, its style of operation, and the application of resources. Peter Drucker is said to have first posed the question that has become the basic question of all strategy planners, "What is our business?" The owner/CEO should not look at his or her business simply as a convenience store, or a parts distributor, or an electrical-equipment manufacturer. Although these names provide a general description of business activities, they fail to provide detailed insight into the real function the business serves and how that function fits in with other businesses, both direct and indirect competitors. Remember, the ultimate intent is to develop a strategic plan that will help achieve personal and corporate objectives, and a strategic-planning process that will ensure survival of the business in the face of changing conditions. This intent benefits from a detailed description of the business. A key part of the description should be outlining the nature of the services provided to the customer so that the alternatives available to the customer are clear. A convenience store sells food and household items to consumers. The service is the sale of goods and by defining the goods the competition from supermarkets, hardware stores, and so on, is indicated. A second issue is the definition of the unique features of the business that allow it to be competitive. For a convenience store, that definition is contained in the word *convenience*: it is a local store, usually open many hours a day, which meets customers' needs for convenience in shopping, especially for emergency items at odd times. The description should not be long, and it should not be so specific that it includes every minor activity. Explicitness actually is more dangerous because of what it excludes than what it includes. The description is not just to ensure that the business appears in the correct section of the Yellow Pages; it is to cause the owner/CEO to think more closely about the business, the way in which it earns money, and its possible competition.

Style of operation refers to the factors that define the business's personality. In chapter 2, examples of illegal or immoral businesses were quoted to indicate extremes of business personality. Other factors that distinguish businesses include:

1. Time horizons and continuity: is the business intended to operate for many years without major changes, providing continuity of service to customers, or is it to be opportunistic, offering the latest services?
2. Growth or stability: is growth an important objective, both personally and for the business?
3. Stature in the area or industry: is the business regarded as a leader in some respects—high-quality services, respected corporate citizen, staff training, broad range of services?
4. Management style: is the management responsibility highly centralized or are responsibilities delegated broadly?
5. For larger companies with several lines of business, how are they related? Do they represent an attempt to integrate vertically from raw materials to end user, or do they exploit unique strengths such as a good sales force handling noncompetitive lines of medical supplies?

As indicated in chapter 2, for most small businesses, there is no question that the owner/CEO has to make all his or her resources, whether financial, personal, or skills, available to the business. However, as also mentioned in chapter 2, there are enough people who wish to limit their contributions of resources in some way that including this in the definition of strategic logic is worthwhile. Many people become executives and managers for others, providing their time and skills but no investment. Others contribute their time and money, hiring the skills they need to operate the business. And a third group invest in a business and let others manage the investment. Another important issue related to the utilization of resources is the willingness to make sacrifices in the name of the business. It is not unusual to read stories in newspapers and magazines of some small-business person who attributed his eventual success to a willingness to put everything into the business. In fact, there is some indication that this dedication of resources is more important than the absolute amount of resources available.

The owner/CEO ought to consider these and other examples when developing the strategic logic to be used as the decision criteria during strategic planning. The elements of the strategic logic are not decision criteria in the sense that they are quantitative parameters to be met or exceeded. They should be unambiguous statements of some necessary conditions that the business should meet in order to satisfy the personal needs and objectives of the owner/CEO. For most owner/CEOs, the statements will be closely linked to the current operation of the business, but as the strategic planning process goes through several cycles, changes will be identified that bring the business operations closer to the owner/CEO's more clearly stated objectives. This evolutionary process is one of the keys to continuing success in making the business more rewarding to operate and ensuring its survival in changing circumstances.

Examples of Strategic Logic

Examples of strategic logic for two companies are provided. The first is a small management-consulting company, about eighteen months old, founded by a group of experienced executives with a variety of backgrounds in computer systems and consulting. The elements of their strategic logic are to:

exploit highly specialized knowledge of the application of computers in sales and marketing;

provide a full range of services from problem-definition to final system implementation;

limit staff growth strictly;

change markets quickly if necessary; and

be pragmatic about the role of the company (if good job offers are received consider them seriously).

These factors cover many issues in the operation of the business although only one can be called restrictive, the strict limit on staff growth. In fact, the company does what many other small consulting companies do: it subcontracts specialized tasks to other consultants if the scope of the work of a particular assignment requires skills beyond their staff's ability. The first two factors identify the special skills that the company wishes to exploit to distinguish itself from others and to justify good billing rates to clients. In particular, the specific statement that the company will undertake to implement its recommendations is a major factor in distinguishing it from other management consultants. From time to time, disillusioned clients complain that consultants lack practical experience or just push paper. For management consultants, offering implementation is a relatively high-risk approach that the principals presumably thought about carefully when establishing their objectives and strategic logic and were able to reconcile with their personal attitudes toward risk. The final two factors reflect a very pragmatic attitude about the role of the business in the lives of the principals. Computer know-how is not so unique that it will ensure market share indefinitely even though it is combined with lengthy executive experience in sales and marketing. If necessary, the business will change markets to exploit its computer and management experience elsewhere. Also, if a satisfied client does suggest that the implementer of a recently installed system might like to manage its operation on a full-time basis, the other principals are aware that the offer will be given serious consideration and that the company and its operations may have to be changed as a result of the acceptance of such a job offer. This reflects detailed attention to the needs of the individual actors during the development of the company's objectives and strategic logic. By doing this in advance, the principals ensure that later changes in the strategic plan to accommodate resignations of key individuals will be smoother that they otherwise might be.

The second example is the strategic logic of a well-established, privately held manufacturing company with international sales of about $30 million per year in a highly competitive industry. Several of the company's key products are based on trade secrets. The factors in this company's strategic logic are to:

guard the trade secrets securely;

provide excellent customer support;

maintain a healthy company with good growth, a sound balance sheet, stable or growing market share, and an excellent management team; and

sell the company at an appropriate time.

The first two factors represent the way in which the company distinguishes itself from competitors. The trade secrets do not cover manufacturing processes or product features that represent high value added to the company but they do represent an obstacle to newcomers trying to enter the markets with similar products. They also add some mystique to the products which is exploited in the sales literature. However, this element of the strategic logic could be dropped without much impact on the company's strategic plans. The president has stated that providing excellent service to the customers is the most important feature of the company's style of operation. They provide applications engineering, fast response to requests for special products, fast response to orders, competitively priced products, high-quality products supported by extensive reliability and performance data, and an active quality-control staff. This element of the strategic logic has been very important in determining the detailed strategic plan.

The third factor satisfies two important issues for the owner/CEO and the other investors and principals. First, it reflects a certain conservatism in managing their investment that in turn reflects some aversion to risks. Second, it is a sound approach to enhancing the value of the company to a potential purchaser. The details in the statement define more closely what the principals meant by "a healthy company"; they need not have been included in an explicit statement of strategic logic but the definition of *healthy* should have been noted somewhere. Market share and growth are attractive features of a company to a possible purchaser. A sound balance sheet reflects good management and also encourages a purchaser. The excellent management group ensures continued healthy operations and is another attractive feature when outsiders appraise the company. In this case, the president encouraged his senior managers by delegating responsibility and authority, involving them in major decisions, and providing bonuses and stock options linked to corporate performance. The final factor is a highly personal decision on the part of the investors designed to meet personal objectives that have not been revealed. They were not in a hurry to sell, and maintained excellent security during several enquiries in order not to cause harmful rumors in the company. The company was acquired recently.

Neither example addresses the assignment of resources to the business. The manufacturing company's logic does not define the business clearly: it relies on the trade secrets as a partial definition but there are no indications of the special features that cause customers to buy their products or the nature of the competition. Selling the company is a style of operation and justifiably included in the strategic logic. It is not a personal or a corporate objective, but an approach to satisfying a need for financial security. It is valuable to include it in the strategic logic because it is a key part of reconciling personal needs with owning and operating the business and any strategy must recognize this. Since it is included in the strategic logic, it is part of the decision criteria to be used in selecting the most appropriate strategy.

Many small businesses should consider adding a strategic-logic element that includes the development of a successor to the owner/CEO. This is good insurance in the event of some personal disaster and also limits any tendency by the owner/CEO to build a monument from the business.

Development of Corporate Objectives

At this point in the planning process, in some respects the difficult work is over, at least until the review of the objectives or the start of the next planning cycle. Now the owner/CEO is in more familiar territory considering the operations of the business and setting objectives. Some may not have formal objectives but all will be able to name some objectives if asked. Good strategic planning requires careful selection of corporate objectives, and for the small-business person, the best objectives are those that are compatible with the individual's objectives, so the business can become the means for achieving personal objectives. Setting corporate objectives requires a good look at the existing business and participation by executives and managers.

The planning process from here on is based on repetition of the same general cycle: set objectives, develop ways to achieve the objectives, select the most appropriate way, and detail that way. Before long, numerous objectives will have been identified, but for the moment consider only the major ones that drive the whole business. The rest will be handled later in the strategic planning process, most likely during the development of program plans. The selection of corporate objectives from many alternatives also requires decision criteria. This is where the hard work that went into identifying personal needs and attitudes toward risk, translating the important needs into personal objectives, and developing a strategic logic is rewarded. These determinations act as the decision criteria. Later, corporate objectives will be combined with the strategic logic to form the decision criteria to be used in evaluating the alternative plans.

The Importance of Objectivity

The flow of the strategic-planning process so far has been from abstract, subjective issues to concrete, objective issues. Personal needs and risk tendencies are highly subjective, but running a business has to be objective. Customers, competitors, banks, and tax authorities will certainly view the business objectively and subject it to rigorous tests. Failure to pass most of the tests will damage the business and could damage the individuals in the business. Therefore, the corporate objectives must be selected with due regard to the strengths and weaknesses of the business, what can be achieved with current and anticipated investments, and what can be achieved in current and anticipated market and economic conditions.

An important way to secure objectivity is to discuss the business with others, starting with the executives and managers, and including experienced staff members when possible. Next, discuss the issues with outsiders such as professional advisors and members of trade associations. This can be done by direct contact with owner/CEOs of companies that are not direct competitors, although even direct competitors are pleased to talk in generalities about the conditions in the economy and market and about the problems of small businesses. Professional advisors and trade associations are also helpful. The conversations will help ensure that the business objectives are not set unreasonably high or unreasonably low.

A general caution is to seek positive objectives as major corporate objectives. There will be plenty of negative objectives—to reduce scrap, limit sales expenses, eliminate branch B, and so on—during the detailed planning process, as barriers to achieving the positive objectives become apparent. Establishing positive goals and seeking ways to achieve them is usually more satisfying and provides greater motivation to the owner/CEO and the employees than seeking out problems and ways to eliminate them. The owner/CEO will want to communicate the corporate objectives to the executives and senior managers, and they will respond favorably to challenging, positive goals. Their response to goals like "eliminate management weaknesses" will be ambivalent at best and could be damaging to the business.

Although continued emphasis is placed on maintaining a sense of reality, this does not mean that the search for alternative goals should not be wide-ranging, including possibilities that at first appear unrealistic. The famous question, "what if . . . ?" should be asked many times. Ask what could be achieved if some barrier such as limited working capital were removed. Mentally try to remove limits on the business. Discuss the hypothetical possibilities with the people in the company and outsiders. There is always a chance that a barrier is not as high as perceived, or that it can be circumvented. The exhortations to objectivity apply to the final selection of the objectives, not to the full range of exploration performed while searching for alternatives.

Quantifying Objectives

Where possible, quantification of the objectives is essential. Objectives that refer to finances, time, people, and physical items like new products are readily quantified. Other objectives such as image and quality are more difficult to quantify. Attaching numbers to an objective provides a way of measuring progress; it is not a substitute for the objective. Later events may force a change in the numbers without a change in the objective; this is a change in the way progress is measured. There is no need to attach a single number to each objective. In fact, it is frequently better to use ranges or limits for objectives, since it is difficult to predict events with the accuracy that justifies setting a single number on an objective.

An example is setting an objective to achieve a market share of 10 percent to 12 percent within three years. This range may appear very precise when considered against the scale of up to 100 percent, but it is not so precise when considered against the scale of the business: an 11-percent market share is the average and the range is almost 10 percent on each side of the average. Imagine planning to achieve a market share of 10 percent to 20 percent. The average is 15 percent and the range is about 33 percent. How can investment planning, production planning, cash flow, and the other important issues be addressed meaningfully in this case? Planning for a 10-percent market share will leave the company without the capacity to satisfy a 20-percent share if it is available; and planning for a 20-percent share will lead to severe financial problems if only a 10-percent market share is available. Planning for a 15-percent market share faces both problems. The time limit "within three years" is less precisely stated but is probably still a viable statement of the objective. The detailed planning will quickly reveal whether that is a conservative objective or what the military call a stretch-objective. If it is very conservative, then perhaps the number of years should be changed to two, but if it is a demanding stretch-objective, consideration should be given during the review stage to the penalties, if any, of failing to meet it, and changes made if necessary.

Some quantified objectives should include firm limits. Usually these are restrictions on the ranges of financial parameters. For example, an employment agency may set an objective of a return on sales of 3 to 5 percent with the 3-percent figure as an absolute limit which, if approached, requires strong management action to defend by increasing sales and reducing costs.

Examples of Corporate Objectives

There are many examples of corporate objectives. Table 3-1 gives examples divided into four classes: financial, sales, physical, and other. Any of the numerous ratios used by accountants could be used as objectives, but since many of them are related, there is little benefit to be gained by setting targets for them all. Later, in the detailed evaluation of the alternative strategic plans, pro-forma accounts will be created that allow any desired ratio to be calculated. It is usually best to concentrate on the major ratios; most companies include at least one target for growth and one for return in their corporate objectives. Service businesses with relatively little capital usually speak of return on sales while manufacturing companies with lots of capital tied up in plants and equipment speak of return on investment or return on assets, the latter more often when the economy is down and cost reductions are required. Growth rates can be set absolutely as growth in revenues from 7 to 10 percent per year; or as ratios of growth in revenues to place the company in the top quartile of companies in the industry; or as limits—growth in revenues to exceed last year's figure. The latter is only realistic for companies in their early years of operation although it has been achieved consistently for periods of ten to fifteen years by some companies (see the *"Inc. 100"* list of small businesses published by *Inc.* magazine every May).

Table 3-1
Examples of Corporate Objectives

Type of Objective	Example
Financial	Return on assets (ROA)
	Return on investment (ROI)
	Return on sales (ROS)
	Net worth
	Revenue growth
	Earnings growth
	Inventory
	Accounts receivable
	Working capital
Sales	Sales growth (units, dollars)
	Market share
	Market-share growth
	Number of products
	Number of new accounts
Physical	Geographical coverage
	New plants
	New field offices
	New products
	New processes
	Withdrawn products
Other	Product-service quality
	Corporate image
	Industry leadership
	State-of-the-art technology
	Established technology

Targets for inventory and accounts receivable go through phases as the economy cycles from good to bad. In good times, they receive less attention than sales and growth targets. In a recession or a period of high interest rates, they become more important when companies need the money tied up in inventories and accounts receivable.

Parameters that are not used as objectives are still important management tools. The number of turns of inventory per year is becoming popular as a management tool to measure the effectiveness of many functions in the company in a direct manner. The number of inventory turns is the ratio between annual sales and the average inventory for the year calculated as twice the sales divided by the sum of the starting and ending inventories for the year.

Sometimes accounting ratios become hypnotic and their significance is lost behind the numbers. This is exacerbated if the parameter is dignified by making it a formal corporate objective. For instance, a small manufacturing company sought consulting help to resolve its problem. It was seeking modest growth but was in a highly competitive industry with a history of cyclical performance. The company's sales had cycled from about $7 million to about $10 million per year. The consultants were asked to advise the company what new products to acquire or develop in order to achieve its corporate objectives. In fact, avoiding cyclical growth was not on the list of objectives but achieving a contribution margin from each new product greater than 35 percent of the product's sales price was on the list (contribution margin is sales minus variable costs). The project was not successful for either the consultant or the client since every product suggestion foundered on the contribution-margin test. The more proposals failed the test, the more important the contribution margin became until the original problem was almost forgotten. A better approach would have been to reexamine the corporate objectives, especially the contribution-margin objective, and determine whether there were any penalties in varying that one. Also, the company had made a tacit assumption that new products could help break the cycle but had no evidence to support it. This was a case of the right question asked in the wrong way, partly because the impact of selecting certain corporate objectives was not thought through.

Many of the sample objectives given in the physical and other sections of table 3-1 can be quantified. What percentage of new business is expected from establishing manufacturer's representatives in New England? What percentage of products need to be replaced in order to maintain a market share in the packaged-goods business? What is required to scale up production of the new engineered plastic from the pilot plant to 5,000 tons per year? How low must the return rate from customers be in order to be the best manufacturer of integrated circuits?

The references to technical status are important for many companies. Several well-known major corporations including Digital Equipment Corporation, Intel Corporation, and Xerox Corporation underwent amazing growth from founding to the present with a heavy emphasis on advanced technology in their corporate strategy. Many other companies have been successful following more conservative technology strategies. A distinguishing feature is the entrepreneur's attitude toward risk since advanced technology by definition involves working on the edge of what is known. A second distinguishing feature is the company's access to capital since advanced technology can be very expensive to develop. Fortunately, for those companies interested in advanced technology, many venture capitalists are also interested because a successful investment offers very high returns.

Communication of Objectives

The corporate objectives eventually chosen—they should be a limited number, eight or ten at most—will be the driving force for the strategic planning and also part of the decision criteria along with the strategic logic for selecting from alternative plans. They should be written down and communicated to the people who will be responsible for the detailed strategic planning. The document should be as short as possible. Keeping it short is good discipline, ensures that the meaning is clear, and encourages people to read it and think about it.

Reconciliation of Corporate Objectives with Personal Situations

After establishing corporate objectives it is often advisable to wait a few days before reviewing them in the light of what you now know about your personal needs, objectives, and risk tendencies. As discussed in chapter 1, the assets of a small business frequently represent an extension of the owner/CEO, who tends to look at the business as the only way to achieve personal objectives. If this assumption is to be validated in practice, the corporate objectives must be compatible with the owner/CEO's personal needs, personal risk tendencies, and personal objectives. Ensuring this compatibility may be the most painful part of the whole strategic-planning process outlined in this book.

Sources of Conflict

Figure 3-2 shows how conflicts can arise. This flow diagram looks complex but is actually a highly idealized version of the objective-setting process. The personal risk tendencies help select directions and approaches that satisfy personal needs through personal objectives; personal risk tendencies and personal objectives help form the strategic logic; and the strategic logic helps select directions and approaches that satisfy personal objectives through corporate objectives. In reality, the process is much more complicated, with many false starts as different directions and approaches are considered and as the understanding of the subjective factors is improved. The attempt to show a smooth flow from subjective issues to objective issues is also highly idealized. It is quite likely that subjective biases and feelings will intrude into steps that should be objective. The diagram does show that there are many routes through the process; each can lead to different outcomes. Therefore, it is not unreasonable that conflicts can occur when the outcomes bear little resemblance to what was anticipated at the beginning. In the worst case, the conflicts may appear to be unresolvable, with no obvious way of reconciling personal objectives with business objectives, at least not without major dislocations. Some owner/CEOs who started the strategic-planning

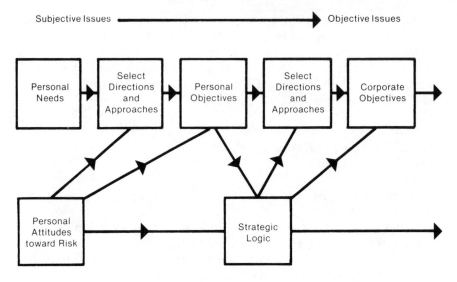

Figure 3-2. Determining Compatible Personal and Corporate Objectives

process so hopefully and put so much effort into it may abandon the process as unworkable. The insights they have gained about themselves and the capabilities of the business to satisfy them may discourage further efforts. The person seeking significant increases in net worth from the travel industry but only having enough resources to operate a campground must stop and consider the situation. The example quoted should not be regarded as an impossible conflict, but certainly the owner/CEO has to take a closer look at the results of the self-appraisal, in particular the risk tendencies and willingness to make personal sacrifices now for future gain.

The situation is even more complex when one takes into account the passage of time. Personal needs may change, at least in emphasis; personal objectives will change as some are achieved and some are dropped as inappropriate or as family obligations change; personal risk-taking tendencies will change with experience as some situations lead to a more conservative approach and some to a more confident approach; and the willingness to make sacrifices will definitely change as time passes and the rewards from previous sacrifices are measured and possibly found wanting.

Handling Conflicts

There are three responses to conflicts between the corporate and personal objectives: compromise, setting priorities, and patience. In most circumstances all three are required. Is it more important to have a certain net worth at retirement even if this means delaying retirement until age 65 rather than at the preferred age of 58? Is it better to stay in the business than to seek new opportunities even if it will not provide the desired level of financial security or prominence in the local community? Can parent and child both be provided with satisfying, challenging roles in the same business? Questions like this are difficult, even painful, to answer. If compromises cannot be reached nor priorities set in a reasonable time, continue the planning process. Objectivity is important: if the set of corporate objectives that has been developed is realistic, it will be a good basis for the first strategic-planning cycle, and later reconciliation with personal objectives may be easier when compromises and priorities are more clearly understood. The planning cycle will also be repeated and it should get easier with time. There will be many opportunities to resolve conflicts in later cycles and the passage of time may make some of them easier to handle since the level of awareness of the issues will have been raised considerably. The increased level of awareness will certainly help with many of the more detailed decisions that have to be made later in the planning process. Options that might otherwise have been closed will probably be left open until some of the complex issues have been resolved.

Evolution of Objectives

The first-time planner should expect to modify personal objectives, strategic logic, and corporate objectives several times. This is a normal process that does not reflect any inadequacy in the original conclusions at all. On the contrary, it is a sensible action that reveals that a key ingredient of strategic planning, namely continuity, is present. But patience is required. Too many modifications made too quickly will lead to confusion and uncertainty. Adjustments in an objective such as a change in the desired growth in sales from 7 percent to 8 percent per year are more easily accommodated than changes in objectives such as a decision to use return on sales as the major financial objective rather than return on investment, or the decision to seek growth rather than consolidation. Also, changes made within a few days or weeks of the original statement of objectives are more easily accommodated than abrupt changes made eighteen months later when the strategic plan based on the objectives is being implemented.

Hindsight is a valuable aid in strategic planning. It increases the pool of experience and improves decisions. Yet the first decisions were made honestly after due consideration, and they should not be changed flippantly.

Involvement of Employees

By this stage of the strategic-planning process, the employees shown the corporate objectives will be commenting on them. Each person will have an interpretation of the objectives, colored by the perceived impact on the individual. The interpretation will include an assessment of the purpose, value, and risks associated with each objective. The response that satisfies the owner/CEO's ego would be an endorsement of the objectives with a statement that they clarify the existing situation and set demanding but achievable goals. Objectivity requires that this response be treated very cautiously. The owner/CEO will benefit more from admissions by the staff that some of the objectives create uncertainty or confusion, that some are contradictory, and that some are uncharacteristic. During the explanation process, the owner/CEO must listen carefully for such comments and, if necessary, make changes. To some degree, this is a sales effort to ensure staff participation in the strategic-planning process; it is certainly a motivational process to encourage staff to work toward the objectives.

Care must be taken to avoid polarization during these discussions. The owner/CEO can tell the staff that it is natural for corporate objectives to be modified as new insights are developed and, if this is the first set of objectives ever opened for discussion, there is an excellent chance that they will be improved several times. Of course, the owner/CEO is ultimately responsible for establishing realistic objectives and eventually the discussions will have to be terminated and the set of objectives most appropriate for the circumstances formally authorized by the owner/CEO. When this is done in an open, professional manner, most key employees will recognize that they have had a fair opportunity to comment and will acquiesce to the final decision. The process is evolutionary rather than revolutionary.

Personal Time Horizons

The last important personal factor to consider in this chapter devoted to personal issues is the variability in personal time horizons. A time horizon is set by the length of time into the future that a person can reasonably visualize. Some people have difficulty seeing themselves or their situations more than a few months ahead; some can span a few years; a few can span a decade. This ability varies with age and with the issue under consideration. The owner/CEO should try to establish some feeling about his or her personal time horizon. One way to attempt this is to ask questions concerning key personal issues. How far ahead can you comfortably think about making personal sacrifices in the interests of the business? How far ahead can you consider working seventy, eighty, or ninety hours a week? How long can you accept putting all the profits back into the business? How long can you wait for personal recognition by the trade association? How far ahead can you forecast personal finances—mortgage payments, college fees, support for an invalid parent? For how many years will an objective motivate you? When will it start to become a nuisance, a torment, or an obstacle?

Many of these questions are unanswerable, but thinking about them illuminates the issue of personal time horizons and emphasizes that even firmly held convictions about personal objectives and corporate objectives can change. The goal is to try to bring the frequency of modifications and changes in the objectives into line with personal time horizons. Then, as the planning cycle is repeated, the changes can be made in a timely manner.

Some owner/CEOs may find that their time horizons are much shorter than the planning periods discussed in chapter 7. They face a real problem. Planning for time periods beyond their time horizons at best makes them uncomfortable but will more likely make them feel ridiculous. They will have serious doubts about the credibility of the plan and the value in pursuing it. One answer to the difficulty is to use a shorter time period at first, stretching it with each planning cycle as experience is gained and comfort achieved. The benefits derived from strategic planning far outweigh any artificial constraints set on the details of the process.

Notes

1. David E. Terpstra, "Theories of Motivation: Borrowing the Best," *Personnel Journal* 58 (1979):376-379.

2. Daniel Kahneman and Amos Tversky, "The Psychology of Preferences," *Scientific American* 246 (January 1982):160-173.

3. M. Granger Morgan, "Probing the Question of Technology-Induced Risk," *IEEE Spectrum* 18 (November 1981):58-64.

4. Curt F. Fey, "Putting Numbers Where Your Hunches Used to Be," *IEEE Spectrum* 11 (July 1974):34-40.

4

Practical Strategies

"Those things for which we find words are things we have already over-come."   —Friedrich Nietzsche

Before going on to the next stages of the strategic-planning process, let us discuss some practical strategies in more detail. This is best done by reference to examples. Several major companies are named because some readers may be familiar with their activities. However, unless specifically stated, all the strategies are appropriate for smaller businesses too.

Eleven basic strategy options were introduced in chapter 2. They were divided into three groups: four market-response strategies listed in table 2-1; three scale strategies listed in table 2-2; and five operating strategies listed in table 2-3. One strategy—market segmentation—occurs in tables 2-1 and 2-2. Several of these strategies are not appropriate for small businesses but there are many others that are.

Before describing them in more detail, we must introduce another dimension of the definition of strategy: the corporation. Figure 4-1 shows that there are five levels of strategy found in a major corporation. The market and product strategies shown below the dotted line cannot exist independently of a business-unit strategy except for a single-product business unit serving one market. The business-unit, division, and corporate strategies can stand alone although most companies seek to integrate all the lower-level strategies into the higher levels. Major corporations have several divisions and each division can have several business units. Figure 4-2 shows how the basic strategies suitable for small businesses fit into the lower levels of corporate strategy.

The definition of a corporation is related to its existence as a legal entity. Corporate strategy deals with issues that affect the whole company, establishing its long-term direction, and selecting approaches to meeting broad corporate goals. Defining a division is more difficult but the most appropriate definition here is that a division includes several business units with common interests. The division's role is to optimize the performance of the business units as a group even if that means one or more of the business units has to operate below its capabilities.

The definition of a business unit is most difficult and has attracted much attention from strategic planners who see this as the basic unit for strategic planning. The key elements of most definitions include:

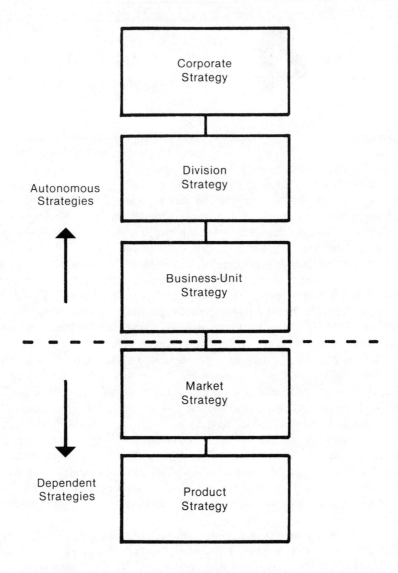

Figure 4-1. Levels of Strategy in a Corporation

the unit has a definite external market;

the unit has identifiable external competitors;

the unit's managers are responsible for its performance;

the unit is a profit-and-loss center; and

	Business-Unit Strategy	
	Product Strategy	Market Strategy
Market-Response Strategies		Late-to Market Strategy
Scale Strategies	Market-Segmentation Strategy	Market-Segmentation Strategy
Operating Strategies	Product-Oriented or Value-Added-in-Manufacturing Strategies	Market-Oriented or Value-Added-in-Marketing Strategies

Figure 4-2. Basic Small-Business Strategies Related to Classes of Natural Strategies and Levels of Corporate Strategy

the unit's profit and loss are measured in real dollars, not using corporate internal-transfer accounting.

These points emphasize that the business unit is in direct contact on a regular basis with the outside world, not just through an occasional sale on an opportunistic basis; the market should have important common characteristics such as related customer profiles, similar distribution networks, and established products. It also emphasizes the presence of established competition and unit autonomy. The definition does not mean that every business unit must have all the functions it needs under its own control; frequently several business units share functions such as research, advertising, personnel, and accounting, but each unit should have autonomy over the use of its resources to develop and implement a strategy within the framework of the divisional and corporate guidelines. The last two points emphasize the need for an unambiguous method of determining the unit's success: profit and loss measured as far as possible in real dollars, avoiding the perturbations of sales and purchases of goods and services among different units, is generally regarded as essential.

A second issue that interests strategic planners is the optimum number of business units to create in a corporation. Having too many business units places great demands on management time while having too few means that some units cover different markets that really deserve specialized attention. Fortunately, most small businesses will not face this problem. It is assumed here that the small business has only one important strategic business unit, in which case the three top layers of figure 4-1 would be merged into one.

Examples of Product, Market, and Business-Unit Strategies

The examples are based on actual occurrences in several industries. They demonstrate clearly the dynamic nature of the strategy-planning process as competitors strive to gain and maintain advantage over each other.

The Calculator Industry: A Product Strategy

Phase 1: Structural Change. The development of the market for electronic calculators is a good example of product-oriented strategies. During the period 1967 through 1972, the electronic calculator was a bulky, expensive product competing with the well-established electromechanical calculators that offered the basic arithmetical functions: addition, subtraction, multiplication, and division. Some of the more expensive models had a memory to store a number and a few more sophisticated functions such as squaring a number. The electronic calculators used the latest in electronic technology which by today's standards was quite primitive. Since they contained many components requiring assembly, almost all of them were manufactured in the Far East where labor costs were less than in the United States. The advantages of the electronic calculator over the electromechanical calculator included noiseless operation, greater reliability, greater portability, battery operation, and extra functions. These factors combined with competitive pricing allowed the electronic calculators to displace the older electromechanical type from the market in just five years.

The electronic-calculator manufacturers quickly had to face competition with each other rather than with the established manufacturers of electromechanical calculators. The strategy chosen by almost all of them was to reduce manufacturing costs, increase production volume, and distribute the calculators to mass merchandisers for sale to consumers. This ensured that selling costs were minimized and also opened a new market—private invidivuals—in addition to the office-equipment market served by office-equipment dealers, which was the traditional market and distribution for electromechanical calculators. The manufacturers of electronic calculators quickly recognized that competitive advantage depended strongly on maintaining high production rates, which required possession of a large market share. With high production, the company benefited from the cost reductions available from the experience curve (see figure 1-1). The more aggressive companies (within a short time there were only aggressive companies left in the business) quickly adopted product-pricing policies that anticipated production-cost reductions consistent with future experience yet to be gained in production (see table 4-1).

Phase 2: Product Diversification. The next phase in the development of the electronic calculator was the introduction of more sophisticated integrated circuits and electronic displays that reduced the number of parts required considerably, in turn requiring less assembly. The results were a dramatic

Table 4-1
Prices and Sales of Four-Function Calculators during the Rapid Growth of the Market

Year	Price	U.S. Sales (units)	Comments
1969	$500	Very small	Each calculator required 50 to 80 components
1974	$20	12 million	Each calcuator required 6 components (integrated circuit, display, keyboard, battery, printed circuit board, and case).
1980	$20	23 million	Also sold 82,000 programmable calculators at an average price of $150.

decrease in the price of the product, and manufacture in the United States became cost-competitive with manufacture abroad. This phase started during 1971 and 1972. The basis for competition in the market for four-function calculators was still market share, high-volume production, and aggressive pricing based on the experience curve. However, the availability of sophisticated integrated circuits encouraged product diversification. First came the addition of numerous functions to the calculator to create what become known as the electronic slide rule. Then came the programmable calculator, which allowed the user to create his own functions.

Both trends quickly produced a broad range of calculators aimed at specialized professional markets such as engineers, statisticians, financial analysts, surveyors, and doctors. These products were higher-priced than the basic four-function calculators and the competitors were able to maintain prices at higher levels for longer periods than in the mass market. The professional calculators were distributed through selective channels including mail-order and telephone sales. Their manufacturers started to add peripherals, specialized software, and firmware (firmware is software permanently contained in read-only memory) to their product lines to sell to purchasers of the calculators. The extra revenues increased the value of the products to the manufacturers but they also depended on having a large base of sold calculators, so market share continued to play a major role in the competitors' strategies.

Phase 3: Marketing Emphasis. In the meantime, the manufacturers of the low-cost four-function calculators modified their strategies. The original market was now saturated and could not be expanded more by further price reductions, even if the manufacturers could afford them. Now the strategy was to exploit specialized packaging and directed merchandising addressing special markets. Calculators for ladies, for children, for the vest pocket; calculators with clocks, watches with calculators, calculators for checkbooks, and so on were developed. Many of these were packaged for purchase as gifts. Others were packaged for use as premiums in sales campaigns. However, the strategy still needs high-volume production, low costs, and mass marketing.

Discussion. The major role played by technology in this example is clear. First, it caused structural change when a new group of manufacturers displaced the established manufacturers from the market in just five years. The manufacturers of electromechanical calculators clearly recognized the threat but they were sure that their dominance of the distribution networks serving the office-equipment market and their extensive and expensive maintenance and repair services would protect their positions. They failed to recognize quickly enough that the electronic calculators needed very little maintenance, so other distribution channels could be used. This meant that individuals started to buy calculators for their personal use and even for work in the office, generating a larger market, bringing down prices, and making maintenance and repair even less important as calculators became throwaway items. Next, technological advances virtually eliminated labor costs from manufacturing costs, meaning that major U.S. semiconductor manufacturers such as Texas Instruments, Inc., and National Semiconductor Corporation could make both the semiconductors and the calculators without cost penalty compared to companies in the Far East. Finally, technological advances allowed the addition of very sophisticated products capable of supporting a higher price, so some companies such as Hewlett-Packard Company and Texas Instruments, Inc., were able to address specialized markets. Today the emphasis is much more on marketing techniques, on discerning specialized consumers who will buy a product directed at them even if they already have another calculator.

It is difficult to claim that this history is typical of the evolution of product strategies, but there are several typical features in it:

the struggle between two different technologies;

the significance of after-sales service in the struggle;

the creation of new markets with a product that is more conveniently packaged for consumers, requires almost no servicing, is priced correctly, and has available distribution channels;

the struggle for market share to ensure high-volume production and maintain position on the experience curve;

the appearance of products with special features for smaller but higher-priced markets; and

the eventual change in emphasis from technological considerations to marketing considerations for the surviving companies.

Large amounts of cash flowed during the first fifteen years of the electronic-calculator industry and undoubtedly many people made a lot of money, but many more companies and jobs were casualties. Even some of the survivors suffered hard times during parts of the development of the market. Both Hewlett-Packard Company and Texas Instruments, Inc., have admitted to losses from time to time in their calculator businesses even though they each tried hard to participate in the professional market, where it appeared that higher prices should guarantee adequate margins.

Energy-Management Systems: A Market Strategy

Phase 1: Mature Market. The market for energy-management systems, part of the larger building-automation-systems industry, is used as the example of market strategies. These are systems used to control many of the services in large buildings such as heating and air conditioning, security, smoke and fire detection, and so on. In the early 1970s, the market was dominated by Honeywell, Inc., and Johnson Controls, Inc. Together they had more than 75 percent of the market. The products were mainly large systems with several hundred to several thousand locations in a building where sensors and controllers were placed. These large systems used what is known as hard-wired technology; that is everything, including the control functions, is permanently established by the equipment installed. They were quite expensive by today's standards—several million dollars per system was not unusual—and were only installed in major buildings. By the mid 1970s, both Honeywell and Johnson Controls had introduced minicomputer controllers that reduced the typical costs by a factor of two and extended the market to slightly smaller buildings that could now be serviced at an acceptable cost.

Phase 2: Revitalized Market. The energy crisis of the mid 1970s quickly created a new demand from potential customers for energy-management systems for use in all sizes of buildings. The technology was available; it only required manufacturers to recognize the need, design the products, price them correctly, establish sales and distribution networks, and enter the business. The new products were mainly small, dedicated systems with several sensor and control points; custom engineering, especially the preparation of special computer software for each application, was reduced to a minimum; and the price was right for many owners and operators of smaller buildings. The systems could perform the traditional building-automation functions but they sold on the basis of cost savings from energy management to the building owner/operator. Among the companies active in the revitalized market was IBM Corporation.

Phase 3: Market Expansion. Traditionally, anything that IBM Corporation does attracts a crowd. Quickly, a large number of companies, including many small businesses and new entrepreneurial companies, entered the market for energy-management systems. However, they extended the market to even smaller systems for smaller buildings using microcomputers to control networks of about five to fifty sensors and controllers. It was soon demonstrated that a large fraction of the energy savings possible in a building could be achieved by using only a small number of control points. These systems are called programmable controllers by the manufacturers. By the early 1980s, IBM, Honeywell, and Johnson Controls had not addressed this market, probably because they did not have the sales and distribution channels to handle many small systems that typically cost less than $10,000; they were more comfortable handling the million-dollar sales.

Discussion. Technology played an important role in this history but not the key role it played in the calculator example. The major factors were the evolution of the market demand as energy prices increased and the recognition of the obvious facts that there are more medium-sized buildings than large-sized buildings and even more small buildings than medium-sized ones. The need for energy-management systems in smaller buildings is just as great as in larger buildings, so the strategy was to satisfy market demand by developing standardized products, correctly sized and appropriately priced, using available technology. The different companies were able to compete in the marketplace by aiming their products at different sectors. This required the development of sales and distribution channels tailored to meet the needs of these sectors. Once these channels were in place, they formed a small barrier against entry by other companies. The energy-management industry presumably has many good years ahead as the uncertainties about energy prices keep customers' attention focused on energy issues, and since there are still many smaller, older buildings without energy-management systems. The opportunities for sales of equipment to larger buildings are more limited; sales will be mainly to new buildings, and their rate of construction depends heavily on the economy.

Local Daily Newspapers: A Business-Unit Strategy

Background. The example of a business-unit strategy is based on the operations of a typical local daily newspaper. The major metropolitan areas are all served by one and occasionally two daily newspapers facing heavy competition from other news media, especially television. These newspapers have large circulations—several hundred thousand copies a day—and large costs for buildings, equipment, and news-gathering services including offices in major U.S. cities and major foreign countries. Many of the newspapers appear to have a gloomy future, especially when it is realized that the populations of most major metropolitan areas are declining and that the people who remain are less affluent and are not targets for heavy advertising.

In contrast, local daily newspapers appear to be in a better position. They are found in suburban areas and smaller cities and towns with populations usually below 500,000. The populations of these areas are growing, and the level of affluence of many is increasing. The papers' circulations are usually less than 100,000, but many advertisers prefer the selective nature of the coverage they gain by using local newspapers. In the mid- to late 1970s, advertising contributed about 75 percent of the revenues, circulation about 20 percent, and the balance came from other sources. Of the advertising revenue, about 5 percent was from major companies advertising nationally, about 25 percent was from classified advertising, and the balance from advertising by local organizations. By judicious use of syndication and news services, the cost of news gathering and feature material can be controlled while still providing broad coverage. However, the costs of facilities, equipment, newsprint, inks, and newspaper distribution are increasing rapidly. This provides a barrier against newcomers entering the business but it also makes daily management difficult. Mistakes in purchasing consumables like newsprint and inks can hurt margins.

Business-Unit Definition. These are not the only problems this class of newspaper faces. The owner/CEO has to decide what business the newspaper is in, and define very clearly the strategic business unit(s) in the company. Newspapers strongly defend their positions as public institutions with freedoms guaranteed by the U.S. Constitution, but the Constitution does not guarantee profitability, so they cannot be operated as public agencies. Several newspaper companies tried to use strategies appropriate to a manufacturing company to maintain profitability. The rationale was that they manufacture newspapers and must control costs to maintain competitive advertising and circulation pricing, and to preserve margins. These are important issues but not sufficient to keep a newspaper in business.

Over the last decade, all newspapers have had to install computer-based systems to handle many aspects of their businesses including handling of classified advertising, circulation lists, text preparation, and typesetting. These major capital investments were justified on the basis of reduced operating costs. Yet the same technology that is helping them is also helping their competitors the radio and television stations, and specialized information services such as the DowAlert™ service (DowAlert™ is a trademark of Dow Jones Radio 2, Inc.).

The dilemma facing the owner/CEO is to determine to what extent the newspaper is a news-information service, an advertising medium, or an entertainment medium. There is no simple solution. The news function is key to the ability to sell the newspaper, but there is competition from all-news A.M. radio stations, broadcast television, and cable television, which now also offers all-news channels. Changes in editorial policy concerning news can help circulation to a limited extent but the competition for the public's eyes and ears is between depth of coverage in newspapers and convenience and rapid response to news from radio and television.

Local newspapers do appear to have some advantage in gaining local advertising as long as they can maintain circulation, a function of their perceived news and entertainment value. All the same, they face stiff competition from free advertising publications, weekly newspapers and magazines, local radio, and more recently, cable television and attempts at specialized electronic advertising services. The rapid spread of cable television in suburban areas is a clear threat since it provides a way of directing advertising quite precisely. The use of electronic advertising services such as AT&T Corporation's experiments with electronic Yellow Pages has been limited as a result of aggressive lobbying by newspapers, but it may still enter the local markets.

Defining the boundaries of the newspaper business unit in the area of entertainment is even more difficult but it could be critical in maintaining the circulation levels so essential to advertisers. Again, the major competition for the consumer's time comes from television in its various forms.

Discussion. Unlike the other examples, it is not possible to derive features of the strategy without studying the situation of one particular newspaper in depth. The most important conclusion to draw from the example is the importance of defining strategic business units correctly. This starts from a clear description of the business of the type discussed in chapter 3 but extends much further into definitions of the markets served, the services provided to the customer, the competition to provide those services from all sources, and the major sources of revenues and profits. The definition of the strategic business unit seeks to establish an integrated business entity in which a change in any major parameter such as product pricing or competitive actions affects all the other parameters. Once established, the owner/CEO must decide what mix of services will be most profitable, how to compete in each service area, and how to make the best use of new technology to control costs. He must determine what the business unit is most effective at, improve its efficiency in those areas, and maintain a watchful eye on the competition, both direct and indirect. While doing this, he must also look ahead at how technological and regulatory changes will affect the newspaper business, and what new opportunities it will provide to the competition. There is no doubt that these changes will force a move to higher-level strategies: one-dimensional strategies—the public institution or the manufacturing company—are not adequate; and two-dimensional strategies appear to have limited usefulness in defending the business in the face of major, perhaps structural, changes in the environment.

Examples of Other Strategies Appropriate for Small Businesses

Innovation

An innovation strategy is applicable to all businesses, but there is clear evidence that it is more easily implemented in smaller businesses, especially entrepreneurial businesses.[1] Major corporations have neither the freedom nor the patience that innovators and entrepreneurs need to improve their chances of success. Major corporations tend to plan and manage every detail, whereas innovators struggle to make reality out of vague concepts and feelings about the right approaches to solving problems. The small company that catches the headlines for being successful against the odds and achieving tremendous growth is an extreme example of the innovation strategy. Apple Computer, Inc., manufacturing personal computers, is an excellent recent illustration.

Donald Taffi and James Quinn, in the articles cited in note 1, emphasize the important personal aspects that contribute to the success of innovation—it is a people-oriented strategy. Some of these factors, along with some of the negative features of the typical entrepreneur follow.

1. Positive characteristics
   a. Self confident
   b. Tremendous reserves of energy
   c. Healthy
   d. Pragmatic
   e. Vision
   f. Strong desire to succeed
   g. Prepared to take calculated risks
   h. Perseveres
   i. Creative
   j. Competitive
2. Operating characteristics
   a. Maintains short-term contingency plans
   b. Seeks advice
   c. Is unwilling to share control
   d. Is demanding of subordinates
   e. Requires tolerance of superiors
   f. Can work in an ambiguous environment
3. Negative characteristics
   a. Obstinate
   b. Unwilling to communicate freely
   c. Disruptive
   d. Unable to delegate authority
4. Needs
   a. Recognition
   b. Achievement
   c. Meaningful tangible rewards
   d. Satisfaction of the seemingly unsatisfiable
   e. Personal expectations

Much is known about innovators, entrepreneurs, and their favored environment, but it is still difficult to plan to be an innovator or entrepreneur and to create the appropriate environment. An innovation strategy is only recommended after a very thorough self-appraisal has been made.

Opportunism

This is a much more common strategy for small businesses. It consists of maintaining awareness of the environment in which the business operates, especially the changing needs of customers, and responding to those changes quickly in order to gain competitive advantage. It is often practiced in the consumer-goods and consumer-services industries, especially the fashion-conscious sectors. The secrets are great sensitivity to changes in consumer attitudes and the ability to respond quickly. Clearly, it is not possible to develop long-range product plans, but it is possible to develop a strategy plan based on opportunism and to ensure that corporate resources are dedicated to implementing it.

Opportunism is not restricted to the consumer-fashion industry. One small manufacturer of patented specialized measurement instruments used in capital facilities for the oil industry had a twofold strategy: continuing business based on industry recommendations as new capital facilities are built, and opportunism, which the owner/CEO calls order-book planning. The company's sales staff and manufacturer's representatives are alerted to seek out opportunities for sale of the measuring instruments in other industries based on the fundamental technology rather than on the instrument design. However, these opportunistic products are not designed until an order for them is received.

Customer-Efficiency Strategy

The objective of this strategy is to understand the customers' businesses thoroughly and to offer products and services that can improve the efficiency of their operations. The greatest success is achieved when the product or service brings about a structural improvement in the customers' businesses, not just an increase in manufacturing efficiency. Structural improvements can be achieved by offering a product or service that reduces the amount of inventory a company must carry, or that reduces or eliminates complex scheduling of the sort that occurs on a production line which makes products with different sets of custom features. This strategy is similar to opportunism since it requires a detailed understanding of the customers' needs. However, it does not require the rapid response that the opportunism strategy does.

Turnaround Strategies

Unfortunately, many small businesses need turnaround strategies to improve corporate performance or to avoid liquidation. If financial difficulties are relatively recent (within a few months) and the problem is one of reduced earnings or cash flow, an operational solution emphasizing improvements in overall efficiency of operations combined with timely strategy planning of the type described in this book should reverse the situation and return the company to normal levels of operation with a sound basis for future strength. This approach relies on the fact that the owner/CEO probably has time to take the necessary remedial steps. If the company has been in financial difficulty for some time, with an extended record of poor or nonexistent profits, unused production capacity, significant debts, and perhaps difficulty in obtaining credit from suppliers, the situation is serious. A careful analysis of the company's assets and potential earning power assuming ideal conditions may indicate that it is not salvageable; and the sensible although very tough course is to liquidate the company. If the analysis reveals that the assets have intrinsic value (that is, if the tools still work, the trucks are still roadworthy, the buildings still have a useful life, and so on), and that good earnings are possible albeit in idealized circumstances, then serious consideration should be given to the immediate implementation of one of several turnaround strategies.

Charles W. Hofer has outlined several tested turnaround strategies and techniques.[2] Usually, when the crisis is recognized, attempts to halt the slide by improving operating efficiency are pointless. Undoubtedly, many steps will have already been taken including closing facilities and employee layoffs. Basically, Hofer recommends assessing the company's current market position using a procedure similar to the Arthur D. Little, Inc. strategy centers or General Electric Company's business-attractiveness matrix. Second, he advocates a review of the company's product and production technologies, if possible comparing them with the competition's. If the company is in a very weak market and technology position, he advocates liquidation or a market-segmentation (niche) strategy; if the company is in fairly good competitive position with supporting technology but in a declining market, he advocates asset reductions combined with some market segmentation; and if the company is in a fairly good competitive position an expanding market he advocates strategies to increase the market share. In the cases he considers, he advocates an asset-reduction strategy if the company's revenues are significantly below fixed costs, and a cost-reduction strategy if the company's revenues are close to or slightly below the break-even point. If revenues are in the intermediate region, a mixed strategy is required with the emphasis varying depending on the ratios between fixed and variable costs. Obviously, attempts to increase revenues are necessary as are attempts to reduce inventories and accounts receivable. These are automatic-reaction strategies, but in this situation time is short. If a basic financial analysis reveals that the company could make money in better times, and because most operating improvements have probably been tried, these turnaround strategies are certainly worth trying although significant effort must be expended to develop the details. Most of the planning tasks outlined in chapter 3, however, can be delayed until the crisis is over. They should then be undertaken to put the company on a sound strategic-planning basis, which will help to eliminate a recurrence of the crisis.

Styles of Implementing Strategy

In this section, the differing styles of management available to implement a chosen strategy are discussed. This dimension introduces the human factor into the strategy-planning process. It is helpful to recognize some of the major implementation styles because they modify the strategies available and provide a more effective set of tools for evaluating and formulating business and corporate strategies.

There are four main implementation styles. None are imprudent if intelligently and deliberately pursued. Not all of the styles are appropriate for all of the strategies identified. The four styles are Caution; Evolution; Revolution; and Aggression.

Caution

Caution can be divided into several subsidiary styles analogous to the well-known techniques used in making financial decisions. However, there is an important distinction between the options available to the financial decision maker and the strategy planner. The financial markets are sophisticated, with a wide range of investments—stocks, bonds, options, puts, calls, and so on—whereas the market for business is limited to products, processes, and business operations that are less freely tradeable. The four subsidiary styles to be used to implement a caution strategy are risk reduction, risk hedging, risk diversification, and risk spreading.

Risk Reduction. Two ways to implement risk reduction are to license technology and to private label products. In both cases, the investor can see the technology implemented at some level of achievement before making major investments in products and marketing, and the implementation will be carried out at someone else's risk. Obviously, licenses can be bought or sold, and private labeling can be done by a manufacturer or a vendor. Many licenses require the purchaser to continue development work to further suit the technology for the proposed use, but the purchaser has the chance to benefit from work already completed and can to a certain extent pick appropriate supplemental technology. The seller of a license gains an opportunity for greater rewards from the investment in the technology and reduces uncertainty in exploiting the technology when two or more different groups are applying it. Well-known examples of licensing are the Japanese companies Matsushita and Sony, who have been actively signing up licensees for their video-cassette-recorder technologies. The more licensees each company has, the more chance that its design will become the ad-hoc standard for the consumer and so displace others from the market. The major American manufacturers of consumer electronics equipment have all taken licenses or made private-label arrangements with the Japanese suppliers to reduce the risks that they will lose credibility in the market by not offering a suitable product. An example of a private-label agreement is the arrangement between Savin Corporation and Ricoh of Japan under which Savin markets Ricoh's plain-paper photocopy machines in the United States. Savin, at the time of the agreement, had limited engineering resources of its own and no manufacturing capabilities but an excellent marketing capability in the office-equipment business. Ricoh reduced their risks in entering the U.S. market and Savin reduced its market risks by using an established product.

On the daily operating level, risk reduction can be achieved in several ways. A good strategic plan incorporating the risk-reduction style will emphasize this. An automobile repair shop, for example, that replaces parts, even if they are repairable, is passing the warranty costs on to the parts manufacturer and reducing the shop's risks.

Risk Hedging. Licensing is also a good way of hedging risks, as RCA appears to have done in the consumer video-player business. They pursued their own design of video disc and launched it into the marketplace, but they also hedged their bets in the video-player market by taking a license to manufacture and sell video cassette recorders, thus ensuring their participation in the market no matter what the consumer chose. There are several other techniques to hedge risks. One is to ensure that new products have the broadest possible range of applications. Another commonly used technique is to develop a modular product line with a range of basic units that can be incorporated into different systems for different applications. Then the investment in developing a particular module has the best chance of making a return. The counter argument is that the extra development and manufacturing costs involved in ensuring that each module can fit with all the others may make the system noncompetitive in the market against custom-designed systems. Nevertheless, this technique has been used successfully by many companies especially those in the instrumentation industry, in which a modular product line typically consists of sensors, actuators, signal-conditioning equipment, communications equipment, computers, and terminals, all capable of configuration into a range of systems with little incremental development cost.

Other risk-hedging techniques include selling to other equipment manufacturers (OEMs) and using bins in production. Companies active in the OEM market derive increased benefit from their investment in product development when the OEMs include their products in systems sold to end users in businesses that their own marketing and sales forces could not reach effectively. Also, the OEM handles the uncertainty of deciding what system features are required. All component manufacturers are, by definition, involved in OEM markets. However, many component manufacturers have another hedging tool available, namely the ability to sort their product into different categories (bins) at the final test stage and to price each category differently depending on performance and other characteristics. As a result, the investment in process technology achieves a greater return.

Risk Diversification. The basic technique in risk diversification for businesses is the same as in finance, the development of a portfolio. Discussions in chapter 1 covered some issues involved in the development of a statisfactory portfolio. The objective of a portfolio is not to move all the investment to the best product but to balance the risks across the portfolio. There are many cases in which mature businesses have an advantage in this regard, since there are many knowledgeable people who can improve the businesses' performances. In a head-to-head technology race, mature technology starts at an advantage but is later at a disadvantage because there is less room for improvement than with new technology. Also, experience-curve effects slow up considerably for more mature technologies, and the new technology gains on and eventually overtakes the old. However, technology businesses can make money during periods of obsolescence when it is clear that there is no need to invest further in a particular technology, that more training and marketing are not necessary, and that the distribution channels are already established. The danger is that the company will not have adequate replacement technology for use when the obsolete technology is finally withdrawn.

Risk Spreading. The final variation of the caution style of strategy implementation is risk spreading. This can be achieved by entering into joint ventures or by establishing product standards. Each partner in the joint venture seeks to ensure that the opportunity for up-side potential is retained during the term of the agreeement. A joint venture can include licensing or private labeling. The use of technical standards in industry is well established as a way in which markets can be enlarged. For example, in the photography and consumer electronics markets, 35-mm film from any manufacturer will fit a 35-mm camera from any manufacturer, or any radio or television set manufactured to Electronics Industry Association (EIA) standards will operate in the United States. However, there are arguments against the use of standards and there are technical and business reasons for being cautious about the use of standards. Most notably, standards can inhibit innovation, since the existence of a standard means that performance improvements are at best limited and most likely prohibited. Nevertheless, standards do spread risk among all the participants in the market. There are several ways in which standard can be exploited. In the computer industry, companies such as Amdahl Corporation, and Cambex Corporation manufacture computers that are compatible with IBM's products. They adhere to the ad-hoc IBM standards and provide users with an alternative source of supply at competitive prices and when IBM's delivery schedules are slow. As mentioned, the formal EIA television standards equalize to some extent the competition in features and functions for televisions and radios, but they by no means eliminate competition. Xerox Corporation, Digital Equipment Corporation, and Intel Corporation have developed a data-communications system for office buildings called Ethernet. They are licensing the approach to many companies—approximately two hundred licenses were granted by the end of 1981, including many to small businesses. In this way they wish to establish an ad-hoc standard for intraoffice communications so that users will be encouraged to install their systems. It is generally agreed that the companies expect to recover their investment by selling office equipment, computers, and peripherals that can communicate over the systems rather than by selling the systems themselves. Some standards are known to be quite vague in certain areas, leaving room for individuality, as in the cases of two communications standards, the S100 standard developed for personal computers and the Institute of Electrical and Electronics Engineers (IEEE) 488 standard developed for computers and instruments.

Evolution

The objective of evolution as a strategy style is to control risks. Many Japanese companies have carefully exploited technology evolution to gain significant market shares in their industries. However, their strategies have been true strategies involving technological and marketing elements. The rapid Japanese penetration of the United States television market, especially for smaller sets, which occurred about ten years ago, came from a recognition that it was possible to sell a second television set to each household in the United States rather than just one large set sold as furniture on the basis of family decision making. In fact, the Japanese saw that it should be possible to sell television sets for each household room as long as they had the mass-marketing competence, television-set designs, and competitive costs to do this. They were able to exploit the private-label strategy through the major mass-merchandisers in this country and developed the process technology to allow them to manufacture reliable sets at attractive costs.

Evolution strategies can be either elective or mandatory. Many companies in the semiconductor industry practice a mandatory evolution strategy. In order to stay competitive in the industry, it is essential to stay on the experience curve and to introduce product and process improvements on a continuing basis. The first manufacturers of any major class of semiconductor product using a new process technology are really better examples of the revolution style of management, but the style quickly changes to evolution. Intel Corporation, the generally recognized innovator of the microprocessor and an early entrant into semiconductor memories, exploits mandatory evolution well. It continuously improves the designs of its components by introducing new layouts and improved process-design rules; it improves its basic processes (for example the high-density MOS (metaloxide semiconductor) process which succeeded original MOS processes); and it improves processing with experience.

More than adherence to the experience curve is required to stay competitive in the semiconductor business. In fact, timing, unexpected technological problems, and competition from other products can lead to difficulties and reduced profitability. The development of the 64k randomaccess memory (RAM) is an example. It was the obvious next product in the semiconductor-memory business after the 16k RAM, but its introduction was delayed by a number of technical problems and aggressive price reductions by the leading manufacturers of 16k RAMS. In addition, the cost of developing the 64k RAM was significantly higher than the cost of developing the 16k RAM. In fact, in the semiconductor industry, the trend is toward ever-more-complex products, many of them with a large software content requiring larger investments from buyers who apply them in their own products. These factors also change the nature of the semiconductor business since the manufacturers must now provide greater support for their products. They face a changing competitive environment as they seek to increase the hardware complexity of the integrated circuits, thus incurring greater cost and possible production delays, and requiring more support for users who find that their hardware is becoming simpler but that their software costs are rapidly escalating. In addition, the users require longer design-in times and seek longer payback periods, forcing the semiconductor manufacturers to extend product lives at the low margins typical of products advanced on the experience curve. Nevertheless, Intel Corporation has maintained its product strategy of leadership by developing and introducing the IAPX 432 (the Micro Mainframe), a 32-bit computer requiring only three integrated circuits in its basic configuration and using an architecture optimized for the software chosen. It is reported to have taken five years to develop at a cost of about $25 million. But it did reestablish Intel's lead of two to three years over the rest of the industry in a high-technology area.

Another example in which following the experience curve is both mandatory and perhaps dangerous is from the fiber-optics industry, where early competition among leading manufacturers such as Corning Glass Works, Valtec Corporation, ITT, and other companies, as well as competition from other communications technologies, have driven the prices of fibers down to levels where even the most optimistic sales forecasts do not really provide adequate returns on the investment made in developing the technology. This occurred even before large markets had been established. The investments already made must be treated as investments in long-range research and development, with the objective of allowing each company to participate profitably in new markets. Both fiber optics and semiconductors have attracted many entrepreneurial small businesses.

Pursuit of the experience curve may be inappropriate if the product loses its value. Another example from the fiber-optics industry shows this phenomenon. Originally, the effort was to produce cost-effective semiconductor (GaAlAs) lasers operating at a wavelength of 0.85 microns, but the trend in system design from 0.85 microns to 1.3 microns changed the business environment. In the longer-wavelength systems, the number of lasers required may be reduced significantly, so the competitive emphasis could change from GaAlAs to higher-cost repairable lasers operating at longer wavelengths and giving higher system performance. Strict adherence to following an experience curve can also blind companies to possible alternative products with better payback. Another example from the semiconductor industry is the application of line-width measure as the tool for monitoring progress. The U.S. Department of Defense (DOD) realized that strict adherence to this measure in the commercial industry was not providing the parts they needed. Commercial manufacturers reduced line width in order to decrease production costs, increase the complexity of a circuit, and gain some advantage in speed. The DOD wanted more emphasis on speed and realized that they must invest in special development programs to ensure that advances in technology provided the improved performance as well as lower costs.

Problems can create many evolutionary solutions. Usually the appearance of a major technological problem results in attempts by some investigators to work around the problem and by some to attack it head-on.

There are many middle paths between these extremes. Also, if one technology requires innovation in another technology to establish its commercial value in the marketplace, then the first technology is at a disadvantage. Perhaps the development of the nuclear-power-generation industry would have progressed more easily if the development of technologies for disposing of nuclear wastes had kept pace with the development of nuclear-reactor technologies.

Revolution

This is the style of strategy management that exploits risks in order to minimize competition and maximize rewards. Most products that are viewed as areas in which the experience-curve style applies started with revolutionary changes that provided the initiator with advantages for some time, while the competition considered the risks involved. Entrepreneurial companies will introduce revolutionary changes because of their general tendency to have lower risk aversion. The Owner/CEO and other actors in entrepreneurial companies frequently have unified interests, there is less well-entrenched investment to defend, and they benefit from the relative ease and rapidity of decision making. Established companies are more likely to concentrate on evolutionary changes by insurance and maintenance investments (see Chapter 5) and portfolio modifications to improve return.

Aggression

Aggression is a well-established style designed to improve rewards by imposing risks on the competition and barring them from a business area. This is usually achieved by inserting hurdles. Some hurdles may be bluffs, such as early announcements of a new-generation product, but other hurdles are real. Product announcements, price announcements, publicized research-and-development programs, and capital investments in new facilities all affect the timing if not the outcome of competitors' decisions. In the late 1960s and early 1970s RCA Corporation, General Electric Company, Inc., and Xerox Corporation all left the computer business as IBM Corporation introduced new products and demonstrated that significant capital was required to stay in that business. Later in the 1970s, Intel Corporation, National Semiconductor Corporation, and Fairchild Camera & Instruments, Inc., all tried to expand their product lines into consumer products but eventually withdrew when the specialized competitors such as Casio, Sharp, and Seiko prospered. Both Texas Instruments, Inc., and Hewlett-Packard Company were able to stay in the calculator business because they found a niche: professional and programmable calculators.

Other threats to competition are patents, lawsuits, and obsolescence of a competitor's technology. Polaroid Corporation and Eastman Kodak Company are currently contesting the market for instant photography, and Polaroid is seeking to use its patents as a weapon in a legal suit. Xerox Corporation was eventually forced by a consent decree to license its plain-paper copier patents, which had effectively controlled competition for almost a decade. There have been numerous suits against major manufacturers such as IBM, Xerox, Eastman Kodak, AT&T, and others by smaller competitors trying to use legal techniques to achieve business ends. This has received increasing attention in the press and business journals. Lester Thurow emphasized the leverage that a small amount of money used to initiate a lawsuit against a company investing in a new factory or product can have against the defendant, who must finance the defense as well as interest charges, possible penalty costs, and inflation during the delay while a final verdict is reached.[3] The *Wall Steet Journal* reported on the use of legal research and development by MCI Telecommunications Corporation in the furtherance of its business.[4]

The threat of product obsolescence may be actual or perceived. A case of an actual threat was the displacement of electromechanical calculators and cash registers by electronic ones. A case of perceived obsolescence that was successfully ignored for many years was the introduction of the radial tire into the United States. In Europe, the threat was rapidly made real by Michelin.

The limited life of a patent is important when it unfavorably affects the time to exploit it. This frequently happens in the pharmaceutical industry because of the need to perform lengthy tests before a drug is approved for sale. Process patents, which usually apply to products already in production, do not suffer from this timing defect as much. They are frequently preferred by manufacturers but they are also more difficult to enforce.

In pursuing an aggression style of implementation, the competitor is the usual object of aggression. The cardinal rule is to *take risks against competitors, not against the marketplace.* Then the style is one of bluffs or bravado, not the lottery that can occur in the marketplace. Implementing aggression is actually a two-step process that can be exploited by a successful owner/CEO. The first step is to decide to enter the business, followed by selection of the aggressive route. Competitors will see the selection of an aggressive style, but since they do not know why the aggressor reached the decision to enter the market so aggressively, they are uncertain of the best response. In fact, there is clear evidence that entrepreneurs affect the environment in which they operate by their decisions. This is probably also true with aggressive management. James N. Buchanan and Alberto Di Pierro contend that, "In a very real sense, the entrepreneur creates his own opportunity set and the act of choice enters a new world that unfolds with choice itself.''[5] Jean-Pierre Ponssard discusses the value of information in competitive situations and describes how even perfect information does not necessarily help the possessor in all situations, leaving the use of bluff and aggression as effective tactics in management.[6]

Table 4-2 summarizes the characteristics of the different styles of management.

Characteristics of Strategic Planning Concepts
Appropriate for Small Businesses

There are several general strategies frequently adopted by small businesses. There are many viable combinations of these strategies and so many specialized strategies that it is impossible to discuss them all. Yet there are several general statements that can be made about strategies appropriate for use by small businesses.

The first and most important statement is to emphasize that a strategic plan, no matter how carefully developed and implemented, cannot replace experience in the management of a business. Companies will do best to stay with their established lines of business and natural extensions of it. The experience and skills of owner/CEOs, managers, and staff are valuable assets, especially if these people have been in the business for some time. It is valuable to question the assumptions behind the conventional wisdom in any business to determine whether they reflect the current situation, but it is also sensible not to make capricious changes without careful consideration of the reasons.

Another natural limit on the effectiveness of strategies is set by the personalities of the executives and key managers of smaller business. Ideally,

Table 4-2
Summary of the Different Styles for Implementing Strategy

Implementation Style	Possible Tactics
Caution	
Risk reduction	Licensing, private labeling
Risk hedging	Licensing, modular products, contract manufacturing
Risk diversification	Portfolios
Risk spreading	Joint ventures, product standards
Evolution	
Elective	Many
Mandatory	Experience curve
Revolution	Entrepreneurial activity
Aggression	Bluffs, escalating investments, lawsuits, making products obsolete.

the owner/CEO should be forward-looking and able to maintain a broad perspective. The chief operating officer or general manager does not need such a long time horizon since that job requires detailed attention to current activities. These ideals are rarely met but little progress will be made in strategic planning and implementation if the senior executives are unable to place the activities into perspective with their daily workload. The owner/ CEO should look for these limitations during the strategic planning process. Fortunately, personalities are not always problems; in many cases the owner/CEO will identify personality strengths that can be utilized in the business strategy, for example a production manager with tremendous attention to detail could be the basis of a strategy to develop high-reliability products for sale to the U.S. Department of Defense.

The characteristics of a good strategic plan vary with the level of sophistication of the strategy selected. These levels are discussed in more detail.

One-Dimensional Strategies

A one-dimensional strategy selects a natural strategy (chapter 2) that fits the company's strengths and appears to have the best chance of meeting corporate objectives. The selection process requires development of a clearly stated set of corporate objectives, evaluation of the business's strengths, and evaluation of the appropriate natural strategies. A good strategy is one that closely matches the business's strengths; whose major points can be summarized in a straightforward manner; that can be easily reduced to implementation plans; and with which the owner/CEO feels comfortable. The advantage of a one-dimensional strategy is its naturalness, which makes it readily understood and easily communicated. The disadvantage is its one-dimensional nature, which largely ignores the impact of competitors or major changes in the environment. The one-dimensional strategy works well in favorable economic and market conditions with little or moderate competition. It does not provide substantial assurance against competitive and environmental changes—the threats to survival. It is incorrect to assume that adopting a one-dimensional strategy takes little effort. Identifying and implementing the correct strategy takes time and effort. Once a one-dimensional strategy is chosen, its effectiveness can be improved by improving the efficiency of operations, but that is usually the only improvement possible unless the strategy is replaced.

Two-Dimensional Strategies

A two-dimensional strategy is specially formulated for a business. It may use a natural strategy as its base but it seeks to reach the corporate objectives by exploiting corporate strengths and competitors' weaknesses. This is the competitive-advantage concept attributed to McKinsey & Company in chapter 1. A good two-dimensional strategy identifies the key success factors in the industry; matches the company's strengths against them, making changes in company operations if necessary; invests in the strengths; identifies the competitors' weaknesses; and attacks those weaknesses from a position of strength. The advantage of the resulting strategy plan is that it explicitly recognizes the changing industry and competitive environments, and prepares the business for survival as these factors change. The disadvantage is that there are more sophisticated strategies that seek to change the environment in the favor of the planner, and that can be used against a two-dimensional strategy. A two-dimensional strategy can be made more effective by improving operating efficiency and by regular reviews and update of the strategy.

Three-Dimensional Strategies

The three-dimensional strategy seeks to do everything the two-dimensional strategy does but adds steps aimed at changing the industry environment and the key success factors in favor of the planner's company. In this way, not only are corporate strengths arrayed against competitors' weaknesses, but corporate weaknesses are masked and competitors' strengths downgraded. Companies that practice this level of strategy usually must prepare for a response in kind from the competition and responses from regulatory agencies, politicians, and public-interest groups. This is the most sophisticated level of strategy, the most difficult to formulate and implement, and the most difficult to compete against if properly planned and implemented. Most smaller businesses would be well advised to implement this level of strategy cautiously. Yet, smaller businesses can utilize a three-dimensional strategy if the owner/CEO perceives a definite opportunity to change the environment or the key success factors; the successful high-technology entrepreneur does this in launching his or her company.

Discussion

A good strategic plan achieves corporate objectives and gains and maintains strategic advantage over the competition. In many industries and many companies, the emphasis is on operating efficiency to ensure profitability, and, by striving to increase efficiency on a continuing basis, to achieve higher margins than competitors. The strategic plan tries to go beyond this and to identify the market sectors, products, manufacturing processes, and sales and distribution channels built on a company's strengths and to exploit the competitors' weaknesses. These are the areas of corporate effectiveness which prompted Peter Drucker to comment that it is more important to do the right things than to do things right.

Notes

1. See Donald J. Taffi, *The Entrepreneur: A Corporate Strategy for the '80s* (New York: AMACOM, 1981), pp. 13-23; and James Brian Quinn, "Technological Innovation, Entrepreneurship, and Strategy," *Sloan Management Review* 20 (Spring 1979):19-30.

2. Charles W. Hofer, "Turnaround Strategies," *Journal of Business Strategy* 1 (Summer 1980):19-31.

3. Lester C. Thurow, "Is the Economy Strangled by Our Laws?" *Inc.* 3 (June 1981):11.

4. Bernard Wysocki, Jr., "Battling Big AT&T, Little MCI Keeps On Landing Sharp Blows," *Wall Street Journal* 198 (September 28, 1981), pp. 1 and 22.

5. James M. Buchanan and Alberto Di Pierro, "Cognition, Choice, and Entrepreneurship," *Southern Economic Journal* 46 (January 1980):693-701.

6. Jean-Pierre Ponssard, "On the Concept of the Value of Information in Competitive Situations," *Management Science* 22 (1976):739-747.

5 Strategy Formulation

"God will not suffer man to have a knowledge of things to come; for if man had a foresight of his prosperity he would be careless; and if he had an understanding of his adversity he would be despairing." —St. Augustine

The objective of this chapter is to present the tasks necessary to formulate strategies for a business. Figure 5-1 illustrates where strategy formulation, the first part of the research phase, comes in the overall strategic-planning process. The end product of the strategy-formulation tasks is a short list of proposed strategies to be subjected to closer evaluation, and tentative plans for their implementation. This is the first part of the detailed planning work although the tentative plans at this stage are no more than general ideas of what needs to be done to implement each strategy. The tasks discussed in this chapter are:

1. an analysis of the business as it exists today, (the situation analysis);
2. an analysis of the environment in which the business operates;
3. approaches to reduce the complexity of the problem without losing important details;
4. identifying discrepancies between the current state of the business and its desired state as expressed by the corporate objectives;
5. formulating the strategies; and
6. recording the results.

Situation Analysis

The situation analysis emphasizes the business and its interactions with its environment, including competitors. The process should be straightforward and is not designed to uncover any major surprises, since most of the data are already known to the owner/CEO. As usual, the emphasis is on objectivity. Features that may be associated with structural change should be highlighted. The results of the situation analysis should be recorded, but much of the information needed is already written down in accounting, production, sales, and customer records, and so on. The final document should be as concise as possible. It will be valuable in the next stages of strategic planning, and even more valuable during the next planning cycle

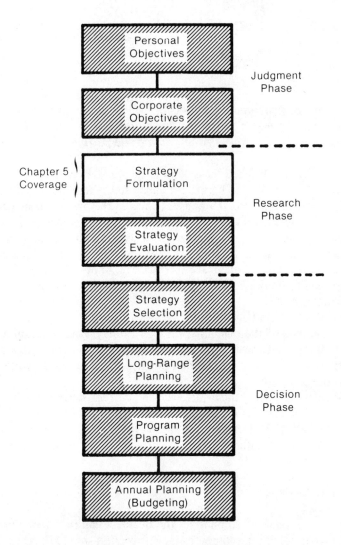

Figure 5-1. The Strategic-Planning Process for Smaller Businesses (Chapter 5 Coverage)

since the situation analysis need only be updated, not redone. Since it is part of the support structure behind the strategic plan, it can be reviewed later to analyze both successful and poor decisions.

Define the Boundaries of the Business

The major boundaries of a business include the following.

1. Geography
2. Products and services
   a. Currently offered
   b. Planned
3. Customers
   a. Population
   b. Characteristics
   c. Buying patterns
   d. Distribution

Geographic Coverage. Geographic coverage should be unambiguous, but it still requires careful definition. Does a resort motel in Viginia Beach serve only Virginia Beach, the southeastern portion of Virginia, or the mid-Atlantic states? An examination of the home addresses of guests may help resolve that problem. A better solution is to consider the range of advertising used to promote the motel. If the sign on the property is the only advertising, then perhaps the geographic area served should be defined as two blocks each side the intersection of 27th Street and Atlantic Avenue. Also, if the motel offers several services such as a bar, a restaurant, meeting rooms, and so on, the geographic area may differ for each service offered.

Products and Services. Listing the products or services offered should be the easiest task of all unless there are ambiguities in the use that the customers make of them. Are people buying baking soda for baking or as a deodorizer? Is a purchase of silverware for personal use or as a gift? The list includes statements of product sales, profitability, and maturity. There is no need for the owner/CEO of a variety store to attempt to list each product and its profitability individually; they can be grouped in major groups and treated that way. The only exception to this would be a small number of specific products that dominate sales or have high margins. Calculating profitability can be difficult, especially for a company with many products. There appear to be as many different ways of doing this as there are people who have considered the issue. The major problem is the appropriate assignment of overhead costs. A second problem is ascertaining the true price received for the product. It is often some sort of average if the company has a price list with price breaks at different volumes. What about returns? How are they charged against the cost of that product? Finally, how are the costs of inventory and accounts receivable handled?

The best approaches at the beginning of the strategic-planning process are to group products and to use a consistent accounting method. Later in this section, the drawbacks of average costing and pricing are discussed. As long as the owner/CEO is aware of the drawbacks and their possible impact, the averaging approach is viable. In fact, it is the only thing to do in many businesses to limit the planning process to acceptable dimensions. Any evidence that averaging is not presenting the true picture for a major product or group of products should immediately be followed up and a more detailed evaluation of those products performed. It is helpful to include planned products and services on the list since they will help during the later evaluation of the discrepancies between the current situation and the corporate objectives.

Products typically have a finite lifetime. Even the buggy whip eventually went out of production. The typical life cycle of a product is shown in figure 5-2. It is helpful to place the business's main products on such a life-cycle curve. Since the lives of different products differ, one type of product may be obsolete before another introduced in the same year reaches maturity. Placing a product on the curve requires consideration of several characteristics. *Embryonic* products are either high-technology products or they are so new that most people have not yet heard of them. The growth period is fairly obvious as the sales volume increases rapidly, but it often includes growth in the number of suppliers. As the market becomes saturated, the less-profitable suppliers drop out; this is the *shakeout* phase. By now, the design and production of the product should be well established. The *maturity* phase is one of reasonable stability, of established suppliers selling established products to a primarily replacement market, with growth linked to general growth in the gross national product (GNP) or to the growth in the population for many consumer products. The *aging* phase starts when other products enter the market; and *obsolescence* occurs when the market disappears or the technology is outdated. The general shape of the life-cycle curve can usually be established without precise sales figures although such figures are very useful elsewhere in the planning process. These and similar timing issues are discussed later in this chapter.

Customers. Evaluating the customers is more difficult than evaluating products and services, but is very important since customers keep the business operating and a thorough understanding of their needs can provide opportunities for future growth. Some characteristics are immediately obvious: does the business rely on a few customers or on many? If there are many customers, do a few dominate the sales? Are the customers mainly anonymous or are they known? Do they form an homogeneous group with similar needs and buying habits? Is it more profitable to serve some customers than others because they place large orders or shipping is less expensive? Have there been major changes in the clientele lately—either major new customers or lost accounts? Do some customers demand special services or special features? Which factors are key to success in gaining cus-

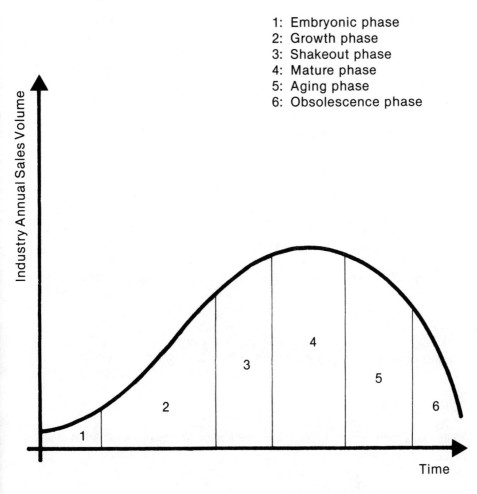

1: Embryonic phase
2: Growth phase
3: Shakeout phase
4: Mature phase
5: Aging phase
6: Obsolescence phase

Figure 5-2. A Typical Product Life Cycle

tomers and making sales? Collecting data on a limited number of major, known customers is straightforward since it only requires contact with them and an examination of the sales records. If the majority of customers are anonymous, collecting data requires a market survey focused on the customers. Surveys vary widely in cost depending on their scope and depth. They are usually performed by a specialist company that develops a questionnaire, tests the effectiveness of the questionnaire with a limited number of interviews, modifies it where necessary, and then administers it to a larger number of actual and prospective customers in order to develop a profile of the typical customer based on a statistical analysis of the results.

If the business covers a wide geographic area, an analysis of the location of the important customers is helpful. Advertising and sales campaigns can be directed more effectively; sales personnel, representatives, or distributors who are lagging behind the rest can be encouraged to greater efforts; unprofitable areas can be eliminated, and distribution channels can be optimized.

Expanding the Boundaries of the Business. Occasionally, business persons view boundaries only in terms of their specific businesses without regard to related businesses or sectors that they do not serve. The first step is to establish the boundaries of the business under consideration and then to expand the definition to cover closely related, unserved sectors. This is less important for the definition of geographic coverage than it is for products and services. Companies will proudly tell you that they sell 70 percent of the widgets used in domestic refrigerators manufactured in the United States. But what if the same widgets, or a similar version, are used in commercial refrigerators, freezers, washing machines, air conditioners, and other similar goods? They may only have 7 percent of the total market for widgets in the country, lagging far behind a potential competitor in terms of total widget production. If that competitor decides to sell to manufacturers of domestic refrigerators, the first company may face severe competition, almost certainly started with price decreases from the new entry.

Company Operations

The main company operations that should be included in the situation analysis include the following.

1. Staff
    a. Skills
    b. Experience
2. Technology
    a. Product
    b. Process
    c. Operating
3. Cost Structure
    a. Value added
    b. Experience curve
    c. Inventories and accounts receivable
4. Financial Aspects
    a. Profit and loss
    b. Balance sheet

      c. Sources and applications of funds
      d. Cash flow
5. Strengths
6. Weaknesses
7. Historical performance (reasons for changes)

Staff. Staff is placed at the top of the list because the best plan will never be successful unless the staff is capable of implementing it. In practice, the plan is usually adjusted to include specific staff strengths and weaknesses. No plan should be so stringent and restrictive that it can not tolerate occasional human error and common human frailty. The most important staff are the executives and managers; their skills, experience, and performance should be thought about carefully before recording them in the situation analysis. In many companies there are key individuals who have specialized technical or market knowledge and experience. Their importance to the business must be assessed. Can they be replaced if necessary? Does someone have such a unique skill that only he or she can perform a certain task? Production lines that rely on an "Old Annie" or her cohorts to make a particular adjustment are not unusual. Are the skills required by the business available locally? Is the staff aging? Is there a high turnover? The answers to these questions have a direct bearing on the ability of the company to be competitive in its industry and market area.

Technology. All manufacturing and some service companies should examine their technological base. This can be conveniently divided into product technology, process (manufacturing) technology, and operating technology. Is the technology new or is it mature? The life-cycle theory described earlier for products also applies to technologies. Incidentally, the life cycle of a product may differ from the life cycles of the technologies used in it and its manufacture. Operating technology refers to items such as computers and office equipment used in the business. Does the small manufacturing company use computer-aided design or computer-based mailing lists? As discussed in chapter 4, technical innovation can quickly change an industry. All products, processes, and operating technologies are susceptible to structural changes as well as incremental improvements. One way to determine whether a structural change is a possibility is to consider the maturity of the technology and the rate at which incremental improvements have been made. If it is a mature technology and incremental improvements have been infrequent in recent years, then the only major technical change is likely to be an innovation leading to possible structural changes. If the technology is obsolete, then the innovation has already occurred somewhere—this follows from the definition of obsolete.

Cost Structure. The analysis of the cost structure of a business provides a baseline for formulating and evaluating detailed strategic plans. The standard analysis technique is cost accounting to establish pricing. The value-added technique recommended here uses the same basic accounting data formatted in a different way. The result illuminates the strengths and weaknesses of the company in a different and well-quantified manner. Figure 5-3 shows this process. Note that basic functions like purchasing are included. In many companies, the ability of the purchasing department to acquire the right materials and services at the best price makes the difference between profit and loss, but few companies look at their purchasing departments as sources of leverage in a competitive market. Every company that needs large amounts of energy for its business—those manufacturing glass, ceramics, certain classes of chemicals, and so on—is in this position. Many companies regard research and development as a cost center and many who would like after-sales service to be profitable actually have a cost center there too. It is not necessary that all the steps be the direct responsibility of the company; distribution and final sale to the customer are often through other facilities. In some industries, there are specialized businesses, for example contract manufacturing or manufacturer's representatives, that perform only one of the steps. Yet it is very helpful to know the full cost structure of the product or service even if the company only plays a small role in the total process.

Table 5-1 gives the cost and value-added structures for a hypothetical manufacturer of four-function electronic calculators. The value-added calculations include the assignment of overhead to each function in the company. For simplicity, the same overhead factor has been used for all the functions. Manufacturers of inexpensive calculators have increased the fraction of value-added created by their marketing, sales, and distribution compared with several years ago, when the value added by R&D and manufacturing dominated.

The experience curve was discussed in chapter 1 and illustrated in figure 1-1. If the manufacturer has made only a few of a new product, then each doubling of experience comes quickly so production costs should decrease rapidly. However, for mature products using mature process technology, doubling the cumulative production volume takes much longer and cost reductions are correspondingly harder to achieve without innovation. This has already occurred in the electronic-calculator industry, and emphasizes the need for the companies still in the business to change their strategies from high-volume, product-oriented strategies to a market-segmentation strategy.

Inventories and accounts receivable are specifically singled out for consideration because of their role in limiting cash flow. As will be seen in chapter 6, cash flow is the most useful way of distinguishing between com-

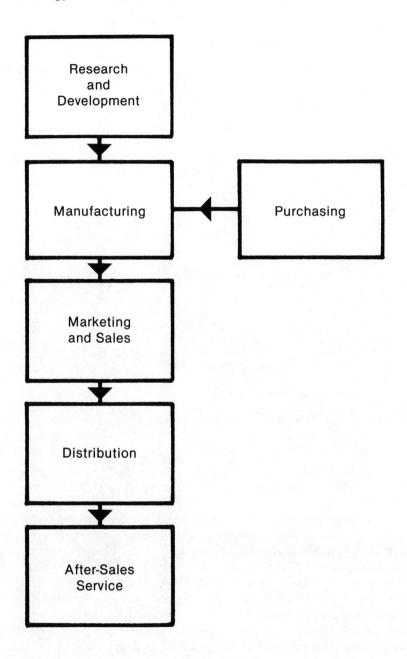

Figure 5-3. Major Cost and Value-Added Functions in a Manufacturing Company

Table 5-1
An Example of Cost and Value-Added Analyses

Cost Element	Cost (dollars)	Margins	Value Added[a] (dollars)
R&D[b]	0.20	—	0.32
Purchasing	0.30	—	0.48
Manufacturing			
parts 3.25			
labor 1.00			
total	4.25	—	6.80
Marketing/sales	1.00	—	1.60
Distribution[c]	0.75	—	1.20
After-sales service[d]	0.14	—	0.22
Manufacturer's margin[e]	—	1.33	1.33
Totals	6.64	1.33	11.95
Manufacturer's sales price			11.95
Store[f]	—	3.00	3.00
Store sales price[g]			14.95

[a]Value added equals cost plus overhead assumed to be fixed at 60 percent for all departments.

[b]The product is a four-function calculator for lefthanded people. It cost $20,000 to develop. Marketing estimates sales of 100,000 in the first year. Management wishes to recover the R&D costs in one year, so the R&D cost per calculator is $0.20.

[c]Distribution is to mass merchandisers such as department stores and discount houses. The costs include packaging, freight, and insurance.

[d]After-sales service is mainly an allowance for returns since little repair work is done. The allowance is about 1.25 percent of the company's sales.

[e]Manufacturer's margin is 12.5 percent.

[f]The stores are owned and operated by other companies.

[g]The selling price of the calculator in a department store. A discount house may choose to take only $1.50 markup and sell the same product for $13.45.

peting strategic plans for small businesses, hence the importance of factors that control it. A useful way of recording these parameters is as ratios to the revenues and total cash flow in a year. Another way is to record them in terms of the number of days of inventory held and accounts receivable due. In this case inventory is related to the production rate and the sales rate, and accounts receivable to the average length of time an invoice goes unpaid. Many companies will need to monitor the amount of money they have tied up by products shipped but not billed. Few companies have problems with bad debts, but those that do should pay close attention to the causes of these problems and steps should be taken to eliminate them. Figure 5-4 shows schematically how these different sinks for cash are related as the parts and materials go through manufacturing to finished goods and on to sales.

Financial Aspects. Cash flow is an excellent decision-making tool in the strategic-planning process as well as an important management tool. The

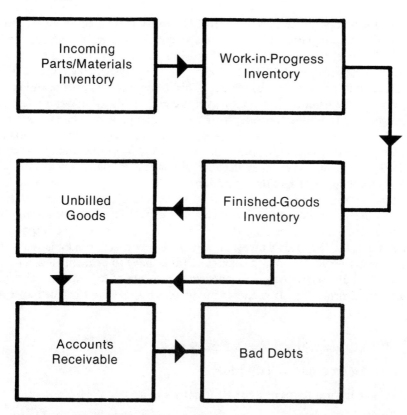

Figure 5-4. The Sluggish Flow of Cash through a Company's Books

standard accounting technique for calculating cash flow is to add after-tax earnings in a given year to the total amount of noncash expenses—mainly depreciation charges for most companies. This may be an acceptable technique for major companies, but it frequently bears little resemblance to the actual cash flow in small businesses. The best way for them to evaluate cash flow is to look at their cash receipts and disbursements on a regular basis—for most companies monthly is about right—and attempt to establish trends. Paydays, tax-payment days, and benefit-payment days (for example, payment of group insurance premiums) will stand out for the really small company while down-payments on capital equipment and materials purchases will probably stand out for somewhat larger companies. Both smaller and larger companies may also see a clear pattern of debt repayment. At the moment, however, the concern is to record cash flows and learn to interpret their patterns.

The standard financial statements, profit and loss and the balance sheet, are important to include. There is no way that strategic planning can lessen their importance to the owner/CEO or to actual and potential creditors such as suppliers and banks. If accounting changes have been made over the years, they should be noted and any such notes attached to the accounts reviewed as well. The final accounting analysis is the statement of sources and applications of funds. This is another way of looking at changes in the balance sheet, but its value comes in identifying the origin of changes in the financial strength of the company. Were changes mainly from outside sources, as loans to support the working capital, as loans to improve the capital equipment, or as loans to support other changes in corporate operations? Were they because of changes in the equity and, if so, how were they used? Did the operations of the company increase the assets through an increase in retained earnings and working capital? If they did, is it possible to decide which particular products and which stages of the value-added structure contributed most? These factors will be important later when the detailed strategy plans reveal how much money is required for their implementation and sources of funds have to be identified. Tables 5-2, 5-3, and 5-4 give sample financial statements of a hypothetical company, Pro Forma, Inc. It is interesting to note Pro Forma's performance in several areas:

Pretax income to sales = 8.2 percent;

Return on equity = 11.9 percent;

Current ratio (current assets/current liabilities) = 2.54;

Ratio of sales to inventories + accounts receivable = 4.88;

Cash flow (net income + depreciation) = $614,300; and

Studying the changes in working capital shows that in 198- Pro Forma, Inc., reduced their inventories by about 10 percent and accounts receivable increased by about 16 percent.

Strengths and Weaknesses. Identifying corporate strengths and weaknesses is another of the planning tasks requiring objectivity. Strengths and weaknesses include tangible items like products and production facilities and intangibles like reputation for outstanding product quality and management talent. The intangibles can be particularly difficult to define, but once correctly identified, they can be utilized very effectively in a strategy. The owners of the small manufacturing company discussed in chapter 3 were able to exploit their management talent during the acquisition process: the acquiring company was impressed by the strength of the management team and its achievements, undoubtedly influencing the acquisition decision and probably the price too. Japanese automobile and electronics manufac-

Table 5-2
Pro Forma, Inc.
Statement of Income for the Year 198-
(*thousands of dollars*)

Income	198-
Net sales	6,788.3
Less	
Cost of goods sold	4,765.5
Selling and administrative expenses	1,131.7
Depreciation expenses	279.6
Interest expenses	53.6
Total costs and expenses	6230.4
Earnings before income taxes	557.9
Provision for income taxes	223.2
Net Income	334.7

turers have carefully developed excellent teams of production engineers in the belief that competition in their industries is governed by the efficiency of production. Many small businesses rely on a strong link to the local community—a sense of partnership and participation—as an excellent marketing strategy. The lists of his company's strengths and weaknesses help the owner/CEO to determine the company's area of greatest effectiveness, which will be an important element in the final strategy.

Historical Performance. The recent performance of the company should be reviewed. A reasonable period to include in the review is the same number of years that the strategic plan will cover. Some of the considerations necessary to determine what the planning period should be will be discussed under timing issues. The review should include a brief commentary on the reasons for any unusual events or discontinuities in the data. If possible, major decisions, their expected outcomes at the time of the decisions, and the actual outcomes should be identified, again with some comments on discrepancies, if any. In this way, the owner/CEO will develop a feeling for his or her performance as a decision maker.

Timing Issues

All plans include objectives, ways to achieve them, and schedules to achieve them. All industries and businesses have natural rhythms which it is difficult to escape from, although it is frequently very desirable to do so. Changing the pace of product introductions can be a winning strategy but usually requires technological innovations and significant investments. Some of the timing issues and important operating cycles to be considered during the situation analysis are:

Product development

Manufacturing

Product life

Technology life

Order satisfaction

Capital-equipment purchasing

Acquisition of staff

Acquisition of capital and loans

Table 5-3
Pro Forma, Inc.
Balance Sheet at December 31, 198-
(*thousands of dollars*)

Assets and Liabilities	End of Year 198-
Current assets	
Cash	147.6
Accounts receivable after provision for bad debts	627.9
Inventories	762.9
Prepaid expenses	5.6
Total current assets	1,544.0
Fixed assets	
Plants and equipment	3,009.5
Less accumulated depreciation	619.1
Depreciated value of plants and equipment	2,390.4
Other assets	
Notes receivable	14.0
Other	111.1
Total Assets	4,059.5
Current liabilities	
Accounts payable	332.2
Income taxes payable	186.7
Current maturity of long-term debt	56.5
Notes payable	13.3
Accrued liabilities	18.8
Total current liabilities	607.5
Long-term debt	648.2
Total Liabilities	1,255.7
Stockholders' equity	
Common stock (500,000 shares at $1.00)	500.0
Capital surplus	200.0
Retained earnings	2,103.8
Total Liabilities and Stockholders' Equity	4,059.5

Table 5-4
Pro Forma, Inc.
Statement of Changes in Financial Position for the Year Ended
December 31, 198–
(thousands of dollars)

Sources and Applications	198–
Source of funds	
Net income	334.7
Expenses not requiring outlays of working capital	
Depreciation	279.6
Deferred income taxes (noncurrent)	21.8
Funds provided from operations	636.1
Issuance of long-term debt	183.4
Sale of surplus equipment	19.2
Total Available Funds	838.7
Application of funds	
Cash dividends paid	25.0
Invested in plants and equipment	579.2
Reduction of long-term debt	59.5
Total Use of Funds	663.7
Changes in working capital	
Increases (decreases) in current assets	
Cash	82.6
Accounts receivable	100.8
Inventories	(76.6)
Prepaid expenses	9.0
Total	115.8
(Increases) decreases in current liabilities	
Accounts payable	7.7
Income taxes payable	10.0
Current maturity of long-term debt	(13.3)
Notes payable	58.0
Accrued liabilities	(3.2)
Total	59.2
Increase (Decrease) in Working Capital	175.0

The Product-Development Cycle. The product-development cycle measures the time required by the company to introduce new products after deciding to do so. In consumer markets, especially high-fashion markets, this time is frequently only a few weeks, and any company that cannot meet that schedule on a regular basis is at a strategic disadvantage. In contrast, parts, instruments, and equipment used in major capital goods like large turbines, aircraft, or power-generation stations can be developed at a more leisurely schedule—up to two years. It is interesting to note that as technology advances and industries mature, product-development cycles tend to slow down. The Digital Equipment Company PDP-4 computer was developed in eight months in 1961 and 1962; the PDP-15, first shipped in 1970, took twenty-one months to develop.[1] A simple explanation is that advanced technology is more cost-effective for users and has advantages in manufacturing, but requires more consideration during product development, often because more complex products are designed as a result of escalating technology.

The Manufacturing Cycle. The manufacturing cycle measures the time taken between scheduling the production of a product or a batch of products and shipment to the finished-goods warehouse. An understanding of this process and the time it takes clarifies the business's responsivity to orders. If the market expands rapidly, how quickly can the company respond with products? If a major order is cancelled, how many products are likely to be in the work-in-progress inventory?

Product and Technology Life Cycles. Product and technology life cycles were briefly described earlier in the chapter. A product's life is usually determined by one of the following factors:

market forces;

technology obsolescence;

economic life; and

inherent life.

Of these factors, market forces are the most potent, followed by technology obsolescence. Figure 5-5 presents the impact of some of the market forces. Manufacturers of electronic calculators are attempting to move from S -curve to S -curve on the market-saturation chart by offering specialized products that create a larger market; for example, calculators disguised as teaching aids for grade-school children. The major Japanese manufacturers of television sets used a similar strategy from about 1965 to about 1973 to increase their sales of sets in the United States (see chapter 4). Selling sets for each room increased the market-saturation level considerably.

Products, especially consumer and low-value commercial products, tend to follow one of several market-acceptance curves. Most make the transition from a restricted primary market to a broad replacement market over a period of years. Many household goods are in this category. Some products make this transition very quickly, for example the electronic calculator, but others are much slower, for example high-fidelity stereo systems. In the latter case, another phenomenon played a role also: the change in public perception of the nature of the product. At first, many products are regarded as luxuries but later are regarded as essential items. A product tends to move quickly from one extreme to the other if it is inexpensive, has few product features, and does not require changes in purchaser habits.

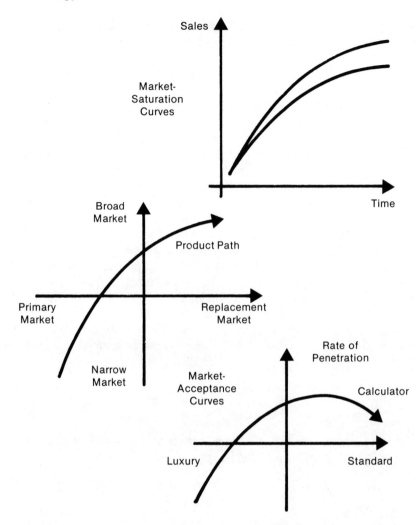

Figure 5-5. The Impact of Market Forces on Product Acceptance

These kinds of product are easier to buy since the purchaser does not have to make complex decisions concerning features or justifying the expense. This perhaps explains the relatively slow growth of high-fidelity systems in the earlier years.

Economic life is determined by either the depreciation policy of the user or changes in the cost of operation that make the product too expensive to use. An example is the trend to replace large eight-cylinder cars for sales personnel by smaller, more fuel-efficient six-cylinder vehicles. Even so, many people keep products in use until they stop operating. If this is a frequent practice, it limits the product life from the vendors' viewpoint since replacement sales are delayed. Vendors also have a different view of the economic life of a product. For the product to be successful, its sales must amortize the investment in development costs, which mandates a minimum life in order to achieve enough sales to reach that goal.

Other Cycles. Of course, estimating the response to rapidly growing markets requires data from other operating cycles: the order-satisfaction cycle deals with the typical time from the placement of an order to its eventual delivery to the customer. Many businesses are not just order-taking operations; they require lengthy business development before an order is placed. The small consulting business is an example, and this business-development time should be included in the measurement of a business-response cycle. It is interesting to note that consulting companies operating in a reasonably strong market usually have a backlog approximately equal in time to the business-response cycle; this is probably true of other service industries such as architectural engineering. Other timing factors that affect the ability of a company to respond to growth are the average time required to obtain new capital or loans; the average time required to hire new staff; and the average time required to build or lease new facilities or major items of capital equipment.

Problems

There are several common problems met during the situation analysis and later stages of the strategy-planning process. For instance:

Standard costing and pricing

Irrational competitors

Product life cycles

Situation dynamics

Strategy alternatives

Lack of data

Standard Costing and Pricing. Figure 5-6 shows what can happen when a company uses standard costing with insufficient consideration of its impact. In this example, the distribution costs incurred by serving 20 percent of the customers are higher than the standard costs used by the accounting depart-

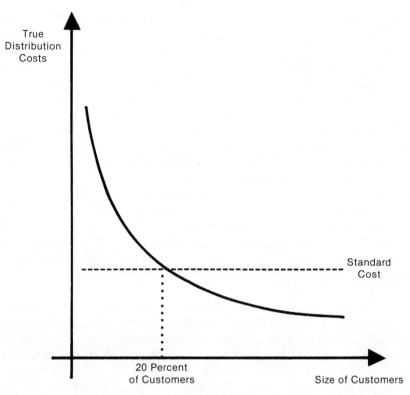

Figure 5-6. An Example of the Problems Caused by Standard Costing

ment. It is important to know this, but the importance varies with the details of the customer population. If smaller customers dominate the revenues, then the true costs of serving the market are being seriously underestimated. If larger customers dominate, then the problem may be only a minor annoyance. Of course, standard costing is associated with standard pricing when the low-cost products subsidize the high-cost ones. If a competitor realizes that this factor is contributing to higher margins than otherwise warranted, he may enter the market with a lower-priced product that is correctly priced. The end result can be a change in the competitive positions of the two companies.

There can be advantages to standard costing based on shared costs. The danger is that a company does not realize that the advantage exists and starts to retreat from certain markets or withdraw certain products without realizing that it actually has a genuine cost advantage and it can defend the market against competitors by reducing prices.

The practice of standard pricing is difficult to challenge. The cost of collecting accurate accounting data on each product to establish its true costs would be enormous for companies with many products. Many companies seek to offer a full line of products in a particular market, which encourages cost sharing across the line; price increases are often made across the line without regard to detailed costs. The strategic planner has to be alert to the problems that can occur and be prepared to perform detailed analyses if they appear warranted.

Irrational Competitors. Irrational competitors can cause serious problems. Newcomers can enter a market with a very poor idea of their costs. The result is pricing that bears little resemblance to the true costs of doing business. Customers may not realize or care about this problem, and the irrational competitor gains a market share at the expense of rational companies. The problem is not restricted to newcomers; established companies struggling to stay in business after extensive losses may decide to cut prices dramatically in order to regain a market share. Again, the impact on the other companies can be out of proportion to the benefits gained by the irrational competitor, which are usually nonexistent.

Product Life Cycles. Determining the position of a product in its life cycle can be difficult in a highly competitive environment. The manufacturer is continually trying to extend a product's effective life in order to derive the greatest value from the investment in it. The competitors are continually introducing new products and modified products in an attempt to limit the useful life of the first product. External events such as changes in technology and changes in operating cost can also limit product life. Failure to recognize when a product is reaching the end of its life can allow competitors to seize the market share. Failure to recognize when the costs of manufacturing and selling products are changing from manufacturing-dominated to selling-dominated as the product matures can affect pricing strategy negatively. Also, failure to recognize when new market segments need a new product provides an unnecessary advantage to the competition.

Situation Dynamics. The complexity of the business situation and the fact that it is in continuous change is another major problem. The only encouragement is that all the competitors find it complex too. Here is where the owner/CEO's risk-taking tendencies become important again. A viable three-dimensional strategy is to destablize the situation by introducing changes and uncertainties, knowing that the competition will have trouble identifying what they are in detail and will have even greater difficulty in determining intentions. There are advantages in choosing to be irrational. One way to do this is to make aggressive attacks on the conventional wisdom in the industry after due thought and planning. The introduction of electronic calculators without establishing a network of maintenance and repair centers is a good example. The established electromechanical calculator manufacturers probably viewed it as an irrational move.

Other Problems. The range of possible strategies can cause problems. Many strategies have been discussed in earlier chapters. Fortunately, they all have common features: namely, they identify the factors for success in the marketplace, identify the company's strengths and the competitors' weaknesses, concentrate resources to build up strengths to support the success factors, and attack competitors' weaknesses.

Finally, lack of data is a problem. The immediate impact of lack of data is to reduce the planner's level of confidence in his or her decisions. Another unfortunate impact is to discourage planning at all. It is encouraging to remember that the competitors are probably short of data also. And the next planning cycle will be easier because the data collected this time does not have to be collected again. (The discussion in chapter 6 includes techniques to use when data are scarce.) The next section covers the environmental issues to be included in the situation analysis.

Environmental Issues

No business operates in isolation from its surroundings. Ideally, a strategic planner should fully define the business's environment in order to establish the business's place in it and to determine the forces acting on the business. But strategic plans are not developed in ideal circumstances and one of the compromises that must be made is to limit the investigation of the environment to issues immediately relevant to the conduct of the business. The major environmental issues that should be included in the situation analysis include:

1. Competitors
   a. Direct
   b. Indirect
2. Markets
   a. Size
   b. Growth
   c. Segmentation
   d. Shares
3. General environments
   a. Economic
   b. Technical
   c. Ecological
   d. Social
   e. Political

Competitors

Try to do situation analyses for major competitors as you would for your own business. It is impossible to achieve the same level of detail, but there are several factors that help. First, all competitors have similar problems. They all work in the same industry, so industry statistics provide general guidance about competitors' performances—but they should be modified to account for special features such as higher market share or more modern production facilities. Also, competitors are all influenced by the same time cycles, so if they plan a new facility or purchase major items of new equipment, it is a good indicator of their long-range intent. Many corporate actions are reported in trade publications and the local press.

This analysis should also be performed for indirect and suspected potential competitors. A local newspaper needs to know as much as possible about the actions of the local cable-television company, for example. They do not compete directly for the subscribers' money but they do compete for advertisers' money.

Markets

A market survey is an essential part of the situation analysis, including forecasts of market growth over a time period consistent with the planning period. The market survey should include market size, historical growth, market shares (both numbers and values of units sold per year) and installed populations, and market segmentation. The estimates of the installed populations help determine competitors' manufacturing costs by examining their experience curves. They also help analyze other aspects of their cost structures. Some companies make more profit on their after-sales service, including sales of consumables and maintenance, than they do on equipment sales. Unfortunately, many companies also lose a lot of money on after-sales service, especially on maintenance. The survey should also examine how customers reach their purchase decisions, since this helps define the key success factors in the market.

An example of changing strategies based on after-sales service is provided by the manufacturers of automated-teller machines used by banks in their lobbies. Until the recent changes in regulatory policies and banking laws in many states, it looked as if the major manufacturers were entering a mature market with sales saturation. The competition was expected to move from product features and price to reliability, not just to reduce inconvenience to the bank and its customers but to enhance the profitability of the manufacturers' after-sales service departments. Currently, there is a rapid expansion in the market for automated tellers as banks install them in many places including supermarkes and liquor stores. Because of the relatively sudden increase in the market-growth rate as the industry has moved from a lower saturation curve to a higher one, delivery time after the order has been placed has also become an important strategic factor. But reliability and minimal service costs are still very important issues with the larger numbers of terminals in use.

The first attempt at market segmentation should reflect the consensus opinion among the main competitors concerning the details of the market. Is it dominated by high-performance, high-price products, or is the largest segment no-frills, low-cost products? Are most purchasers major corporations that include the products in their capital budgets or are they sold to intermediaries for incorporation in large systems? Many minicomputer and microcomputer manufacturers sell their products to manufacturers of office equipment, communications equipment, instrumentation, building-automation systems, energy-management systems, and so on. Later we will discuss the importance of performing a personal evaluation of the market segmentation. This may challenge accepted industry wisdom but it often reveals insights into the market that have not been exploited; hence the popularity of market-segmentation strategies (as indicated in figure 4-2). It is clear that the Japanese television manufacturers segmented the market in a different manner than U.S. companies; in fact they saw a major segment of the market that the American manufacturers either did not see or ignored until it was too late.

General Environments

There are obvious links among the five general environments—the political process affects them all; many people relate ecological issues to social values; and technical advances have impact on the economy and ecology—although the timeframes of the impact vary widely. Economists have established clear links between technical advances and growth in the GNP. There is also clear evidence of unfortunate consequences to the ecology from some technical advances. Despite these links, the separation into classes helps the planner considerably. A brief consideration will allow an owner/CEO to identify the classes that impact the business directly and those that have less immediate impact.

Economic Environment. Usually, the economic environment is paramount. Here, the first action is to divide the issues into general and local issues. The general issues include the perceived trends in the national economy and the industry in which the business operates. If the small business is also engaged in significant international trade, the economies of the foreign countries involved should also be examined; this is not discussed in this book. Local issues include the trends in the geographic areas covered by the business or under consideration for expansion, and the sector of the industry in which the company participates.

Technical Environment. For many small businesses, technical issues are also very important. Here it is possible to be much more precise in determining what should be examined. First, look at the trends in the technologies associated with the products and production processes. If possible, try to determine what the competition is doing. They may have achieved incremental advantages by simple product or process changes that are difficult to dignify with the phrase advanced technology. For some companies, consideration of other technologies that could compete is important. Perhaps the makers of electromechanical calculators would have fared better if they had examined the advantages of electronic calculators more closely. However, knowing what other technologies to examine, knowing what to look for when one does, and having the skills and time to do it are tremendous obstacles, and most small businesses have to rely on colleagues in trade associations and articles in the trade press to alert them to threats that need further consideration. For some companies, an examination of technologies that affect their internal operations is also required, for example the availability of improved computerized scheduling and accounting systems for a construction contractor.

Ecological Environment. Fortunately, ecological issues do not affect most small businesses directly, but if they do, they are usually a major issue because of regulation, and because of the social pressure that develops. Examples of small businesses affected by ecological concerns include service stations disposing of oil and adulterated gasoline; or manufacturers of bottles and containers, printers and distributors, stores, and recyclers of trash in states with bottle bills or container legislation on the books or advocated. Businesses that make or use chemicals obviously must look at the ecological environment.

Social Environment. The social environment includes relatively straightforward items like the demography of the served market area but it also includes complex issues such as changes in personal values. The readily quantifiable issues apply to every business since they help determine the number of prospective customers, and, more importantly, changes in the number of customers. Sometimes a good feeling for the trends can be reached with little effort; plans to open a store to sell children's goods—clothes or toys—should be closely examined if the local school districts are actively closing schools and have plans to close more, especially at the kindergarten and primary levels. Changes in social values are very important to companies selling consumer products and services, in particular those that are fashion-oriented or require discretionary spending. Will the practice of preventive medicine become the vogue for the great majority of the population, and if so, what business opportunities will be created? How will social change affect the readership of the local daily newspaper?

Political Environment. The political environment creates the most heat and very little light. Even so, the impact of political decisions and changes in political ideology as local, state, and federal governments are voted in and out have major effects on business regulation and the economy. Fortunately, most political effects are not immediate. Unfortunately, many of the lasting effects are not what was intended nor what the experts forecast.

Structural Change. One class of force that must be included in any planning process is that which causes structural change. Most changes are evolutionary (incremental) although cycles of alternative advance and retreat superimposed on the evolutionary change are common. A simple example of this is the increase in the GNP of the United States over the years. The GNP is higher today, in mid-1982, than it was three or four years ago, even though the economy has been in a recession for over a year. Evolutionary changes are fairly easily monitored and forecast. The imposition of cycles on them makes the matter more complicated, but reviewing the forces that control the evolution and the cycles can lead to useful forecasts of the general position of the next turnaround point and the magnitude of the underlying trends. Evolutionary changes are fairly easily accommodated in the planning process.

Structural changes, on the other hand, frequently cannot be forecast in any meaningful way, and are usually very difficult to accommodate in the planning process. Of course, if one's company promotes the structural change in the industry, it can be a very effective strategy to gain competitive advantage. Identifying stuctural changes frequently requires challenging conventional wisdom in an industry. It certainly requires careful thought about the true meaning of events that are taking place in the business's environments.

Sources of Data. There are many sources of data, information, and informed opinions on the various business environments. They include professional advisors such as consultants, professional journals, trade journals, major newspapers and magazines, trade associations, colleagues, and experts in the company. Most major libraries can offer information-search services using computer files if the searcher can define his needs reasonably closely. All libraries have a reference section that contains guides to finding information. There are small businesses that will do the searching for you; their services vary from just producing a list of sources through providing copies of the sources listed to providing copies with a commentary on the material. Most consultants will provide this service with the addition of commentary, critique, and recommendations directed at the business's current situation.

Guides to business information include *Where to Find Business Information*,[2] the *Directory of Industry Data Sources*,[3] the *Guide to Reference Books*,[4] *The Standard Periodical Directory*,[5] *The Directory of Directories*,[6] *PROMT*,[7] *The U.S. Industrial Directory*,[8] the *U.S. Industrial Outlook*,[9] to name a few.

Discussion. The objective of the environmental review is not to attempt to develop a detailed description of the current situation in each area and prepare detailed forecasts of their future development. The first cannot be achieved within reasonable expenditures of time and effort, and the second cannot be reliably achieved at all. The planners's goal is to identify the major forces affecting the environment under consideration. Once the forces have been identified, their evolution should be examined and forecasts of possible future changes made. Then the planner should study their impact on his or her business.

An example of a factor that is critical to the U.S. economy and to almost every business in the nation in 1982 is the high level of interest rates. There is little to be gained from personal attempts to make detailed forecasts of interest rates, and not much to be gained from studying the forecasts of experts with political motivations. There are independent experts employed by major banks and financial institutions, academic institutions, and companies who publish forecasts that are possibly more reliable. The individual owner/CEO will gain more benefit from studying their comments on the underlying causes of high interest rates, judging which of these causes will dominate in the future, and attempting to forecast the direction, speed, and general size of future changes in interest rates. Remember, the objective is to determine whether the cost to the company of bank loans in the immediate future is going to increase or decrease, to what extent, and how quickly, not to state dogmatically that the interest rate will be 10.7 percent in December. The impact of interest rates on the operation of the business is clear: cash flow is required to repay the loans; margins are affected; and plans for growth may be constrained. Factors generally thought to influence interest rates include federal-, state-, and local-government deficits, Federal Reserve Bank policy, personal savings, corporate retained earnings, state- and local-government surpluses, personal demand for loans, corporate demand for loans, and liberalized banking regulations. Even this list is reduced by many experts to federal-government deficits, Federal Reserve

Bank policy, personal savings, and corporate demand for loans. Can the government control the deficits? Will the Federal Reserve Bank ease its money-creation policies? Will individuals have sufficient money to be able to save? Will they believe inflation is controlled enough to make savings secure? Will companies continue their demand for loans no matter what the cost? These questions do not always have yes or no answers, but reasoned estimates that look ahead several months to two or three years do exist in the financial pages of major newspapers, major magazines, and responsible trade journals.

Some major forces may not affect small businesses enough to merit further concern, at least in the short term. The planner has to sift through the major forces and their potential impact to determine which are the ones that deserve closest attention during the planning process. Changes in the balance of trade between the United States and Japan are clearly affecting political actions, the exchange rate between the dollar and the yen, and major industries. But if a business is not directly involved in one of those major industries, the balance of trade between the United States and Japan is unimportant. Even in affected industries, the nature of the impact depends on the role of the small business in the industry. A components supplier to U.S. automobile manufacturers is obviously concerned about the increase in imported automobiles, while the dealer in foreign cars is quite happy that imports stay strong.

After the key forces in the environments have been determined and their current status and likely future evolution examined, consider them from another viewpoint. Which forces can have their impacts modified by actions of the business, which can be influenced, and which must be accepted? There may be no need to change or influence any of the forces but those that can be influenced should be identified for consideration later in the planning process. Examples of forces that can be influenced or changed include demographic changes (if the population of school-age children is declining rapidly in the area served by a toy store, consider expanding the area it serves by changing advertising and delivery policies—influencing the impact—or moving the store to an area with more appropriate demographics—changing the impact).

The planner must follow up on forecasts. If he or she believes that interest rates will decline rapidly because of changes in policies of the Federal Reserve Bank, this assumption should be noted and Federal Reserve Bank actions monitored. If what happens differs from the assumption, the forecast must be modified and any decisions based on it reconsidered.

Reduction of the Problem

Classifying Problems

Conserving precious time and resources is vital to most owner/CEOs. This is closely followed in importance by attempts to reduce the complexity of the problems. An obvious solution is to include only the major problems in the planning process, but the problems cannot be divided into major and non-major without first identifying several and using decision criteria to classify them. By adopting the process described here, the problems and decision criteria are identified in a timely and orderly manner. All problems that affect a business's ability to reach its objectives are major problems and must be included in the detailed planning process. Other problems could become major as time passes and they should be monitored. Still others can be safely ignored until the next planning cycle. The review of the environments will reveal issues in each problem category. However, there is another reason for performing the review: it often reveals opportunities that should be included in the planning process. Not every environmental force that is identified as major is a problem.

Finally, structural changes are most often important issues that either become major problems or opportunities. If identified, they should automatically be included in the planning process.

Reducing Complexity

Merge Strategies. There are several steps that can be taken to reduce the complexity of the planning process. The first, which is usually available only to small businesses, is to merge strategies (see figure 4-1). Most small businesses need only develop a business-unit strategy. This will approximate the corporate strategy closely. Later, after experience has been gained, market and product strategies can be developed. But in all businesses these depend for their objectives and decision criteria on the business-unit strategy, so their development is relatively straightforward after the business-unit strategy is established. In chapter 7, market and product strategies will be considered as program plans.

Merge Environmental Reviews. A second simplification can be achieved during the environmental-review stage. The economic, social, ecological, and political reviews can be merged as a review of the markets for the business's products, including a market forecast. These environments all affect the market, so it acts as a proxy for them in the evaluation. Some aspects of the economic environment such as interest rates, labor availability, and inflation have an impact on the operations of the business rather than on its markets, and they ought to be reviewed separately. Also, the reasoning behind any market forecast should be understood to get the best value from it, and this will require some understanding of the interaction of the environments. Unfortunately, preparing a good market review and forecast takes time and resources, but its relevance to the business is immediately obvious, and as a result it is the favored approach for many. It is also valuable later when choices have to be made among alternative plans. Whether a review of the environments or a market study is performed, evaluate only the key parameters in the environments.

Concentrate on Objectives. Another good approach to simplifying issues and problems is to concentrate on the objectives. Issues and problems that appear to be diverting attention from the objectives are probably not important enough to place in the major class. The comment was made in chapter 2 that an unspoken part of the strategic logic for all honest businesspeople is to avoid illegal or immoral activities. However, there is one lesson to be learned from those who do engage in such activities, at least as represented in fiction, movies, and television. Such crooks have well-defined objectives, they know the environment in which they must operate to reach them, and they plan carefully to beat the victims and the law-enforcement agencies (their "competition"). Throughout, they keep their attention focused on the objectives and deal with each issue that occurs from the viewpoint of how it will interfere with achieving their objectives. They appear to plan well, knowing the restraints and working around them to achieve their goals. The technique is laudable even if the objectives and the methods used to achieve them are not.

Discrepancies

The next task in the strategic-planning process is to identify discrepancies between the conditions as revealed in the situation analysis and the desirable conditions. There are three important comparisons:

1. the company's capabilities in each of the identified key factors for success;
2. the company's strengths and weaknesses against those of the competitors; and
3. the current situation compared with the corporate objectives.

There will be discrepancies in each area and the strategic planner's task is to prepare a plan that reduces or eliminates the discrepancies identified in the first and third comparisons, exploits the favorable discrepancies identified in the second case, and minimizes or eliminates the unfavorable ones. The plan will involve risks and the strategy planner has to make the distinctions between avoidable and unavoidable and acceptable and unacceptable risks discussed in chapter 3, so that the final plan avoids the risks that can be avoided and addresses those that cannot.

There is room for creativity in studying the discrepancies. The company may not be strong in a key area for success, for example, numbers of engineering designers; but the owner/CEO may recognize that technology is changing so that computer-aided design systems that the company can acquire will leverage his or her design team and maintain a competitive position. The strategic plan should consider whether the acquisition of a system will improve the company's ability to stay competitive or whether other changes are necessary to close the gap in design engineering. If the value added from marketing, sales, and distribution is going to increase rapidly, perhaps design can be subcontracted to someone else without sacrificing margins.

Similarly, the impact of weaknesses in comparison to major competitors may be minimized by strategies that hasten changes in the industry or change the importance of the established key success factors. Of course, competitors may try to achieve the opposite results. One factor often met is patent protection: competitors who can successfully avoid a patent reduce the advantages held by the patent-holder. Improving product reliability to reduce service calls is a good sales point, reduces service costs, and reduces the advantage held by the competitor with a strong service department.

The situation analysis will reveal features that are not consistent with the corporate objectives. Even the most creative strategy plan may not be able to eliminate all of them. The simplest example is the company with modest growth in earnings and assets that the owner/CEO hopes will produce significant gains in equity. The most likely cause for this descrepancy is lack of objectivity in setting objectives. Now is the time to consider modifications to the objectives although changes should be made carefully, with deference to the effort that went into their original formulation.

The discrepancies should be written down; they are now the driving force in formulating strategic plans. If possible, make a list of priorities, although that is not essential.

Formulate Strategies

This section presents a structured approach to formulating strategies. Unfortunately, this is not a cookbook process. Faithfully following the steps outlined here does not guarantee a good strategy. Rather than regarding the techniques as restrictive, they are intended to stimulate thoughts about a range of possible strategies. As stated in chapter 1, the human factor in the strategy-planning process is noteworthy, allowing people with similar situations and objectives to develop different strategy plans.

A methodical approach does help ensure that all the important issues are covered. It also makes it easier to divide the planning task among several people. Most of the steps discussed here have been introduced earlier.

Describe the Business

This description may differ from the first one developed now that the situation analysis is complete, but it should still be consistent with the statements of personal objectives, strategic logic, and corporate objectives; it is the description of what the business should be after the strategic plan is implemented. The business activities included in the definition are aimed at exploiting the company's strengths and competitors' weaknesses. As far as possible, they should be consistent with establishing a long-term defensible position.

Segment the Markets

The results of the situation analysis help segment the markets. They show which markets are served and which are not, which are profitable and which are not, how resources are shared among them, and how the company differs from the competition in its performance. Customer needs in each market and how best to serve them have priority in the process. The underlying reasons for cost differences among markets and among competitors need diagnosis. The market-segmentation process requires inputs from the market studies and forecasts as well as the cost analyses so that changes in customer needs can be included in the analysis. Also, the market forecasts may reveal market segments not served, or emerging segments. The cost of serving each segment is important and the data have to be analyzed in terms of value added and cost contributions at each major step in the process. Steps with significant shared activity among several products and markets can create strategic advantage as long as the problems of standard costs and standard pricing are recognized and addressed.

Define the Strategic Business Unit

The characteristics of this definition are described in chapter 4. It is among the most difficult tasks even though its results appear to be obvious. Unfortunately, the moment the definition is completed, it starts to lose validity because of the actions of competitors and changes in the environment. The best business unit is an integrated operation in which decisions affect all unit activities. Its definition has two sets of elements: one set binds the unit together, and the other set links it to the attractive market segments. An analogy is the football team in which coaching blends individual skills into teamwork, and the game plan guides the team against a specific opponent. Skills, teamwork, and game plan form a winning team.

Discrepancy Analysis

The results of the discrepancy analysis provide a list of things about the business and the market that either need changing or can be exploited. The best-defined strategic business unit that takes into account the strengths and weaknesses of the business may still not have strong capabilities in all the key success factors for each market segment. The strategic-planning process does not seek to maximize every strength or minimize every weakness. Rather, it seeks the best combination of actions necessary to achieve corporate objectives. The discrepancy analysis, especially the discrepancies associated with key success factors, provides a starting point for several possible plans as the planner selects and rejects approaches to reduce or exploit them.

Discrepancies as Opportunities

The discrepancies are studied and techniques for reducing, eliminating, or exploiting them proposed. These techniques, when reduced to lists or practical suggestions and arranged in an order the business can perform, are the rudimentary strategic plans. Closing the gaps improves effectiveness and efficiency, and exploiting those gaps which are advantages helps improve competitive position. Since the discrepancies have been measured between the current position of the business and the desired position to achieve compatible corporate and personal objectives, closing and exploiting the gaps also brings the business closer to the needs of the owner/CEO. Discrepancies are opportunities available to the owner/CEO to improve his or her business position.

Strategy Formulation

Several possible plans should be examined. It will be necessary to plan through or around difficulties and risky elements. Examples of one-dimensional and two-dimensional strategies that can be used as patterns for formulating custom strategies are presented here; they are mainly for product-oriented companies but they can be generalized to service companies.

One-Dimensional Strategies. Considerable accumulated experience provides guidance on strategy formulation for manufacturing companies. Some of the more successful technology strategies and some of the ways technology can be used in products and production processes are listed below:

1. Some technology-strategy options available to companies
    a. invest heavily in creating new technology
    b. exploit advanced technology
    c. exploit mature technology
    d. fast-follow in technology
    e. insist on proprietary technology
    f. apply technology in products
    g. apply technology in processes
    h. apply technology in services
    i. apply technology to improve efficiency in own business operations
    j. improve company's share of available technology
    k. develop and protect only critical technologies
    l. ensure security of technology base
2. Levels of technology integration into products and processes
    a. know-how
    b. patents
    c. materials (part-processed product)
    d. components (at various levels of complexity)
    e. assemblies
    f. subsystems
    g. systems
    h. systems supported by service
    i. systems supported by engineering
    j. turnkey systems

There are also many well-known ways of incorporating products into a business:

I.   Product offering by type
     a. commodity
     b. differentiated
        1. single product differentiated by performance and quality from competition
        2. multiple products differentiated by performance and quality from each other and from competition
II. Product offering by breadth
     a. product only
     b. product plus limited service
     c. product plus full-line service
III. Product price relative to direct and indirect competition
     a. high, sell on performance, quality, and specification
     b. equal, sell on substitution or system-cost criteria
     c. low, sell on limited substitution criteria

The literature offers some guidance on the different technology-strategy options available to managers. John R. Moore stresses the value of leverage technology. He defines a leverage technology as "that technology which . . . is the key to advantages which justify the product's development."[10] Ideally, one leverage technology should be used in several products, increasing its benefits to the developer. Proprietary technology provides important protection against uncontrolled competition. An even stronger position is achieved when the company also has the financial strength to support the product through all stages of development and changes in markets. Products that do not have a proprietary edge in the market but are still based on high technology levels should offer high value added to the company to defend against competition from underfinanced and entrepreneurial competitors who copy or mimic them.

James B. Quinn describes several possible research-and-development (R&D) strategies available to a company. According to Quinn, the objective of a good research-and-development strategy should be to divide the programs into three areas: areas of concentrated effort; areas of awareness of activities elsewhere by other groups; and areas where it is reasonable to ignore changing technology.[11]

A.J.A. Sparrius discusses several management techniques that can reduce risk in research and development. They are all well known but they must be actively applied in order to derive the full benefit from them in a product-oriented strategy. A list of these techniques would include:

1. Use configuration management of the product/process development (configuration management is a formal process for controlling the development of a product).
2. Limit advances in the state of the art
3. Set a succession of limited objectives
4. Fabricate and test distinct development models and prototypes
5. Perform early and repeated testing
6. Seek incremental improvements
7. Perform parallel developments of alternative product/process solutions
8. Attempt to keep the options open as long as possible
9. Attempt to maintain technological transparency (technological transparency means that modules and subsystems in a product can be replaced by new ones, incorporating new technology when it is available, without affecting the rest of the product).

Although these techniques are all excellent, they do not guarantee success. Further extensive experience shows that the effectiveness of communications between the marketing and R&D sectors is very important, and unfamiliarity with marketing and lack of marketing expertise are major barriers to success. The problem is that the lists of options given here of technology strategies and how technology can be used and incorporated into a business are only one-dimensional, providing a tidy description of the role technology plays in a business, other possible roles that it could play, and possible ways to enhance the return on investments in technology, but providing no real insight into the use of technology as a competitive weapon.

Two-Dimensional Strategies. Figure 5-7 shows the basis of a way to discuss alternative strategies in a two-dimensional manner, recognizing that markets and technologies are interrelated, providing greater insight into the options available, and providing a more sophisticated tool for considering the risks associated with the options. The figure shows in two-dimensional format a company's current position and future opportunities in technology and markets. The company may move from its existing base of products, manufacturing processes, and markets by introducing improved or new technology, by entering expanded or new markets, or by a combination. Square A1 is the base square and represents the company's current position. Each currently successful product line means the company has a specific set of technical and marketing capabilities. Any proposal for new technologies or new markets implies that the company must move from the base square, incurring some risk. A new product that moves the company to square A2 implies the company is willing to handle moderate technology risk while maintaining low market risk. Conversely, a new product in square B1 implies low technology risk but moderate marketing risk. At today's state of development of analytical techniques it is not possible to quantify the axes of this matrix, but there has been extensive research over the years into the reasons for the success or failure of new products. Alan M.Kantrow summarizes some of this work and points out that it is generally recognized that success depends on the attention given to the needs of the marketplace.[13] Changes in markets appear to be more risky than changes in technologies. In this discussion, technology can refer to products or processes. In practice, a product can not exist without product and process technologies. The analogy is a tennis match: it requires a ball (the design) and two players (product technology and process technology) for a match (the product) to occur (exist).

There is usually more than one product in the base square of figure 5-7. These products may serve a range of markets using several different technologies. Any of the standard analysis techniques such as the Boston Consulting Group portfolio-management matrix or the General Electric Company business screen (see chapter 1) can be used to describe them. Most companies' strategy is to limit risks by operating in a number of markets that may range from mature perhaps even declining markets to embryonic

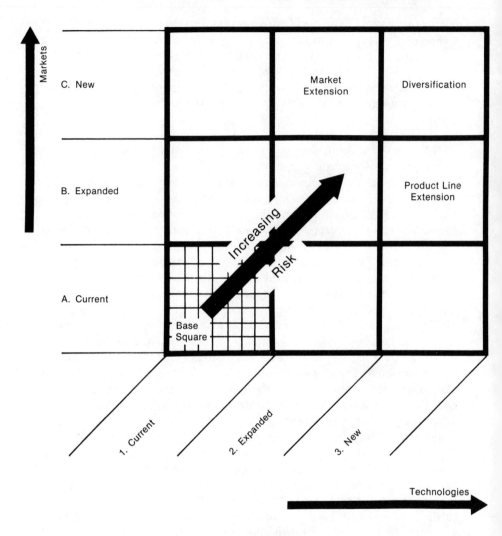

Figure 5-7. The Basis for Discussing Alternative Two-Dimensional Strategies

markets with strong opportunities for growth. They also try to have available a range of technologies appropriate to their current markets so that they have a balance between embryonic technologies with a high level of risk, growth technologies that offer good returns with some certainty, and the lower-potential mature technologies with reasonably certain futures. Often the different products in square A1 should have different product or market strategies in order to achieve the best results for the company. It is well established that the portfolio approach to management reduces the overall risk in operating a business since a relatively predictable result can be achieved by combining a large population of events, each of which is individually uncertain. Nevertheless, care is required, since an unbalanced portfolio of products leads to higher risk exposure and possibly to poor performance. Also, attempts to eliminate risk entirely, such as by limiting technology investments or by limiting market development, usually increase the overall level of risk that a company faces. Reducing technology risk can actually increase market risk by a larger amount, as in the calculator case.

There are several general requirements for all the alternative strategies considered. First, corporate survival is a necessary but not sufficient condition for achieving good returns. Of course, there are circumstances when ensuring survival is of paramount importance, but under most conditions, owner/CEOs are seeking to improve their corporate performance. Next, the strategy must include elements that avoid technical obsolescence or dependence on declining markets since both limit opportunities for profitable operation and remove support for future growth from technical advances or market exploitation. Third, it is important to account for changes in the environments in which a company operates, and for actual and possible changes in competitors' actions. Finally, the strategy must provide a balance between the financial risk of overreaching in the application of new technology and the market risk of not offering cost-effective products or services that are well founded on advanced technology. This balance point will differ for different corporations depending on the risk-aversion characteristics of the owner/CEO and other key decision makers. Each competitor seeks to establish strategies they perceive as having an overall risk warranted by the prospect of appropriate rewards and which matches their risk profile.

The six major two-dimensional strategy alternatives are to

1. Maintain the status quo.
2. Create new base (A1) squares.
3. Insure markets.
4. Maintain markets via technology changes.
5. Maintain technology via market changes.
6. Improve market/technology position.

Maintain the Status Quo. The objective of this strategy is to ensure that the company stays in the base (A1) square. This is a highly desirable situation allowing the company to derive the greatest benefit from its R&D expenditures, and providing the most effective use of investments in sales and marketing organizations. Unfortunately, it is impossible to maintain this strategy in a competitive environment for more than a short time. The problem is that competitors' moves, technology advances, and market changes all cause movement backward relative to the rest of the industry, illustrated in figure 5-8. As can be seen in this 5 × 5 matrix version of the market-technology plot, there are other squares representing the impact of aging technology and declining markets. Except for highly specialized markets such as antiques, many of the new squares in the 5 × 5 matrix do not make sense as technology-market combinations. Travel along the diagonal toward obsolescent technology and petrified markets is a real problem that must be avoided.

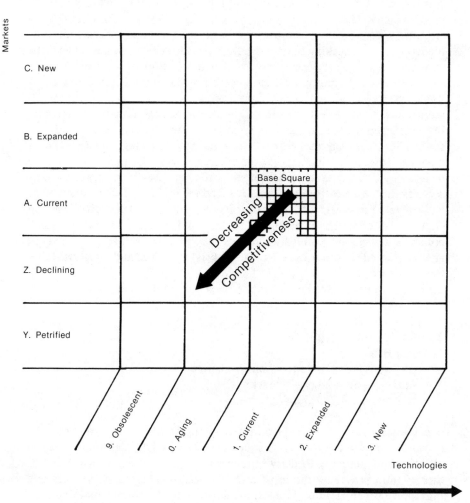

Figure 5-8. Likely Result of an Attempt to Maintain the Status Quo

Create New Base Squares. This strategy option requires developing new marketing and technical capabilities in a company. However, definite risks must be faced as it requires leaving established markets and technologies (see figure 5-9). The objective of the strategy is to create the most beneficial base square with the least risk. It is important to ensure that the appropriate resources—finances, people, facilities, and equipment—are available to facilitate the creation of the new A1 square. Usually there are real constraints in an established corporation and the new square is frequently not far removed from the original. The result is analogous to the case of improving the market/technology position, to be discussed. Creating new base squares is a diversification strategy that differs from a genuine entrepreneurial strategy simply because the new entrepreneur has no established business to help provide stability. This is one of the portfolio-management strategies.

Insure Markets. Figure 5-10 shows this strategy related to the base square. The objective is to invest in technology to insure against unexpected losses of current market share caused by competitive actions or environmental changes. The cardinal rule is insure only against untenable losses such as losses of a market share in major high-margin markets. Attempts to insure against losses in minor low-margin markets are usually not viable. Unfortunately, in many companies the owner/CEO's risk tendencies mean that insurance investments in such technology are delayed or avoided because of real or perceived risks in the investment. The U.S. television manufacturers in the early 1970s struggled for several years with the issue of the best manufacturing approach to meet the changing competitive environment. While they were trying and dropping approaches, the Japanese were engaged in a concentrated effort to automate their television-set production to the greatest extent possible and continued to make gains in the market. It is generally not worthwhile to try to insure technologies against market changes. As pointed out earlier, movement along the market axis involves more risks than movement along the technology axis. Nevertheless, most companies seek to ensure that their markets have sufficient longevity to enable them to recover their investment in developing a technology.

A recent example of the problems that can arise is the magnetic-bubble technology (an innovative computer technology for storing data). A mismatch developed between the timeframes in which the market developed (much more slowly than expected), and the rapidity with which the technology developed, requiring companies continuously to upgrade their technologies to stay abreast of the competition, those developing the magnetic-bubble technology and those developing competing memory technologies such as integrated circuits and magnetic disks. The developers believed that later generations of the magnetic-bubble technology would be

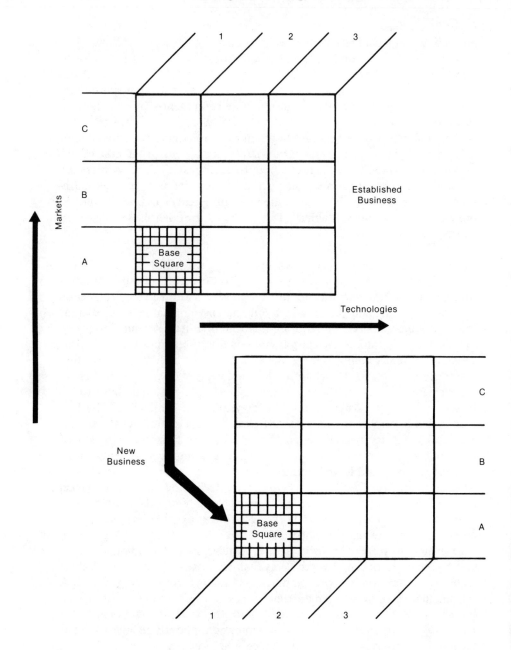

Figure 5-9. The Strategy of Creating New Base Squares

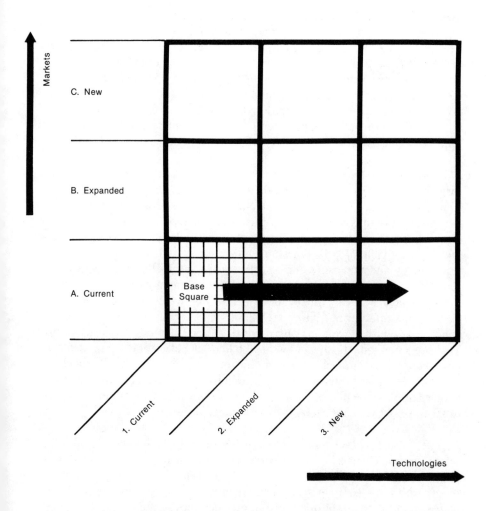

Figure 5-10. Insure-Markets Strategy

more cost-effective and more reliable. In fact, they were chasing a moving target with no clearly defined, addressable market large enough to justify continued development. The result was inevitable. The payback period for the investment increased and the forecast size of the payback decreased, leading to abandonment of the technology by several U.S. companies in 1981.

Maintain Markets via Technology Changes. This strategy is graphically similar to the insure-markets strategy (figure 5-10). The major difference is that the investment in technologies is aimed at increasing return from the markets rather than just insuring against loss. The standard example of this strategy is the experience curve pursued so energetically by integrated-circuit manufacturers. Among others, Intel Corporation has exploited continuous improvements in technology to reduce manufacturing costs and stay ahead of the competition. This approach enables them to maintain margins on new products at acceptable levels for the longest possible time as prices come down, and also allows them to introduce new integrated circuits that offer more functions per unit cost, in a timely manner that keeps the competition off-balance.

Maintain Technology via Market Changes. Figure 5-11 shows the trajectory of this strategy along the market axis of the market-technology matrix. The objectives are to use existing technological resources in expanded or new markets to maximize the return from the technology investment and to establish new marketing capabilities with lower risk than incurred by moving into new technologies as well as new markets. The difference between this strategy and the insure-markets strategy is that this is more aggressive. The 3M Company is an excellent example of a company that has exploited this approach by taking one or more of their basic technologies, for example tape manufacturing, into new markets quite remote from the original concepts when the technology was first developed. Among other activities, 3M is now applying its tape know-how to handling electronic components in integrated-circuit and electronic-equipment assembly. Sears, Roebuck & Company's recent expansion of activities into the financial industry is also a good example of technology maintenance. In this case, the technology is the retail-store network and retailing experience.

Improve Market/Technology Position. Figure 5-12 shows this strategy schematically. This is a basic portfolio strategy in which a company invests in a range of markets and technologies in order to achieve an acceptable rate of return with risks compatible with the owner/CEO's risk tendencies. Companies will seek to establish a range of product lines, some with low risk and comparatively low returns and some with high risk and anticipated higher returns, to offset the increased risk. Large corporations with many lines of business balance their risks among businesses in the traditional portfolio manner. The difference between this strategy and the create-new-base-square strategy is the general relationship between the markets and technologies that can provide an evolutionary approach to achieving the strategy's objectives. However, many companies do make major changes in their portfolios by stepping from the base square to nonneighboring squares.

Discussion. There is a hierarchy of options for the development of a business strategy. The emphasis has been on presenting alternatives in such

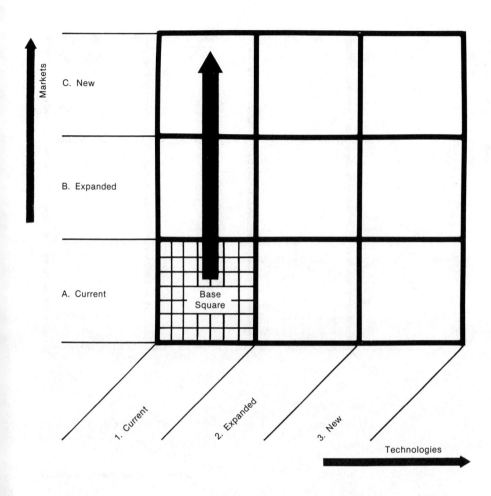

Figure 5-11. The Strategy of Maintaining Technology via Market Changes

a manner that risks can be identified. Unfortunately, significant work is still required to quantify many of the risks, but the hierarchy described here should help the strategy planner build on theory and experience to identify and evaluate the options available. The one-dimensional-technology strategy options, although limited in power, are well known, clear, and represent wisdom based on cumulative experience gained over many years. However, they have limited effectiveness and are regarded as conservative or restrictive by many owner/CEOs seeking revolutionary or aggressive styles of management. Nevertheless, as discussed in chapter 4, although

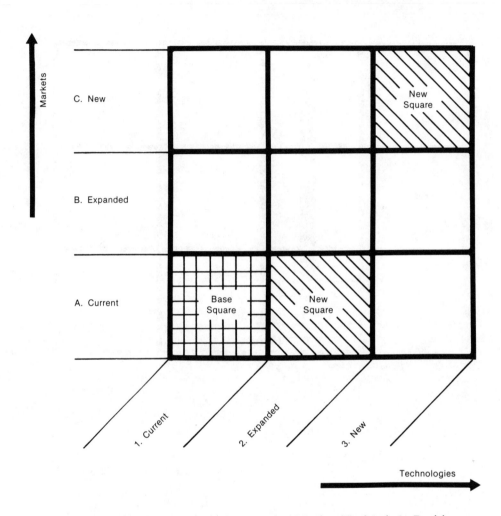

Figure 5-12. The Strategy of Improving Market/Technology Position

entrepreneurial risk taking is required to handle revolutionary change, the conservative approach enhances the chances of continuing success in managing products through the evolutionary and caution styles. Also, revolutionary development can quickly change to evolutionary development.

The two-dimensional market-technology strategy options discussed here are also based on experience. The significant assumptions made—representing the possible impact of four external environments by the markets; the absence of quantitative data on the risks; merging product and process technologies; and formulating the product-strategy alternatives independently of the financial strategies—must be remembered and allowed for in the final selection of a strategy.

A three-dimensional strategy is also developed from experience. This is where the human factor, the "can do" spirit, enters most clearly. In principle, to develop a fully integrated strategy it is best to start here, but this approach is also the most difficult. A more pragmatic approach is to use the one-dimensional or two-dimensional representations as a guide for formulating alternative strategies and then to select the weapons to be used from the third dimension, see chapter 4.

There are several other features worthy of note. Figure 5-13 demonstrates the universal applicability of portfolio strategies and evolutionary styles. However, it also reveals that these two concepts have detailed structures allowing for more refinement in the analysis of strategy alternatives. Portfolios can involve the creation or acquisition of new businesses (base squares) or entry into related businesses (improving market/technology position). Portfolio strategies can be implemented using any of the styles discussed. Most likely, different elements in the portfolio will require different styles for their most effective implementation. Evolution can be divided into mandatory and elective evolution. The distinction should be carefully made in strategy planning since it illuminates some of the ways in which competitors control a company's actions as well as revealing possible ways to control competitors' actions. Also, there is the distinction between insurance and maintenance strategies. An insurance strategy is essential in many situations but it does have real limitations as a basic strategy for growth; maintenance strategies are more appropriate but are certainly not the only option for growth.

Problems in Strategy Formulation

The biggest problem is that strategies can form naturally instead of being formulated in a controlled way. Henry Mintzberg analyzed how strategy can arise and identified three ways:

1. a formal, planned process;
2. an unstructured process; and
3. an entrepreneurial process dominated by one person.[14]

The different ways appear to produce different types of strategy. The formal process (this book describes a formal process) produces an explicit, action-oriented strategy designed to achieve specific objectives and to guide future operating decisions. The unstructured strategy is the outcome of several decisions that exhibit consistency. The decisions may have been

	Maintain Status Quo	Create New Base Squares	Insure Markets	Maintain Markets via Technology Changes	Maintain Technology via Market Changes	Improve Market/ Technology Position
CAUTION						
Risk Reduction	●		●			●
Risk Hedging	●		●	●	●	●
Risk Diversification		●				●
Risk Spreading	●	●				●
EVOLUTION						
Mandatory			●	●	●	
Elective			●	●	●	●
REVOLUTION		●				●
AGGRESSION		●		●	●	●

Figure 5-13. Styles of Implementing Strategy

reached by careful thought, but by starting anew each time; or they may have been reached after considerable argument among the decision makers. In both cases, it is a learning process although it has been referred to as muddling through. The strategy that emerges is backward-looking since each operational decision depends on what was learned from previous decisions. In contrast, the formal process looks ahead at what is required for future decisions. The entrepreneurial strategy is usually unique and depends on the characteristics of one person, the entrepreneur, who is prepared to do things his way and who is confident of the validity of the approach. Entrepreneurs frequently produce such a closely defined strategy that one change in it causes problems.

Unfortunately, intended strategies do not always come to pass. The unstructured approach comes into play in all cases and can introduce modifications in planned or entrepreneurial strategies. People believe their experience is sufficiently valuable that it can be allowed to modify the intended strategy. This is a problem. The value of experience can not be overestimated. However, unless the person is exceptional, experience is uneven in its quality from issue to issue. Strategy planning in the ordered manner described here requires attention to many details to ensure that nothing is overlooked—one reason for adopting the process. The decision maker's experience may lead to a certain decision that affects the intended strategy. The decision may be correct, but this book argues that decisions should be made in the framework of a formal planning process—strategy formulation—to help ensure that they are correct, and that all their ramifications are understood.

The main points to consider during the strategy-planning process are:

the use of the list of discrepancies to focus the strategy-formulation process on meaningful issues;

the fact that the strategic plan will modify the description of the "business I am in" to the "business I will be in after the plan is successfully implemented";

the transient nature of the business-unit and market-segmentation definitions;

the need to examine cost and value added for strengths or weaknesses;

the possible strategic advantage of activities that share costs; and

the possibility that conflicting strategies will form in the business.

For consistency, the business after strategic planning must also satisfy personal objectives, the strategic logic, and corporate objectives. Although evaluation and selection processes will be discussed in the next chapter, it is useful here to perform preliminary credibility checks on the strategic approaches by comparing them with personal and corporate objectives to eliminate any obviously inappropriate suggestions as quickly as possible. It is also helpful to imagine the position of a competitor and think how he would react to the strategy if implemented. Knowledge of possible responses strengthens the final version of the plan. Another useful activity is to examine the impact of possible changes in the environment on the strategy, especially those changes which might occur if some of the assumptions are later shown to be incorrect.

In practice, very few strategic approaches will withstand more than a cursory review. These approaches will be subjected to detailed evaluation in the next stage of the planning process. As a starting point for later steps detailing the plans, identify some of the programs needed to implement the strategic plan. Finally, summarize the strategies in the short list. A standard format can be used such as the one shown in table 5-5. These summaries are the data necessary to start the next step.

Table 5-5
Format for Summarizing Alternative Strategies

Summary Elements	Comment
Business description	What customer needs are served and how?
	What is unique about the business's products and services?
Situation analysis	What are the boundaries of the business?
	What are the company's strengths and weaknesses?
	What is the company's cost structure?
	What is the company's financial status?
	Who are the competitors?
	What are their strengths and weaknesses?
	What are the markets (segmentation, size, growth rates, and forecasts)?
	What major forces are at work in the business's environments?
	What are the key success factors in the markets?
Strategic business unit	What elements bind the business unit together?
	What elements link the business unit to the customers (actual and prospective)?
Discrepancies/opportunities	How does the business situation compare with the key success factors?
	How does the business compare with the competitors?
	How does the current business situation compare with the corporate objectives?
Strategy A	(Identifying name).
	What are its main objectives?
	What level of strategy (one-dimensional, and so on) is it?
	What style of strategy (caution, and so on) is it?
	What are the main programs needed to implement it?
Strategy B	(Identifying name).
	And so on.

Notes

1. Montgomery Phister, Jr., *Data Processing Technology and Economics*, second edition (Santa Monica, Cal., and Bedford, Mass.: Santa Monica Publishing Company and Digital Press, 1979), p. 504.

2. David M. Brownstone and Gorton Carruth, *Where to Find Business Information* (New York: John Wiley & Sons, 1979).

3. *Directory of Industry Data Sources*, edited by William A. Benjamin (Cambridge, Mass.: Ballinger Publishing Company, 1981).

4. Constance M. Winchell, *Guide to Reference Books*, eighth edition (Chicago: American Library Association, 1967).

5. *The Standard Periodical Directory*, fourth edition, edited by Leon Garry (New York: Oxbridge Publishing Co. Inc., 1973).

6. *The Directory of Directories* (New York: Gale Research Inc., 1981).

7. *PROMT* (a monthly publication by Predicasts, Inc., Cleveland, Ohio).

8. *The U.S. Industrial Directory*, edited by Lee E. Elkins (Stamford, Conn.: Cahners, Inc.). Published annually.

9. *U.S. Industrial Outlook for 200 Industries* (Washington, D.C.: U.S. Department of Commerce). Published annually.

10. John R. Moore, "Unique Aspects of High Technology Enterprise Management," *IEEE Transactions on Engineering Management* EM-23 (1976):10-20.

11. James Brian Quinn, "Long-Range Planning of Industrial Research," *Harvard Business Review* 39 (1961):88-102.

12. A.J.A. Sparrius, "Uncertainty-Reducing Techniques in Technological Innovation," *IEEE Engineering Management Review* 9 (September 1981):31-39.

13. Alan M. Kantrow, "The Strategy-Technology Connection," *Harvard Business Review* 58 (July-August 1980):6-21.

14. Henry Mintzberg, "Patterns in Strategy Formation," *Management Science* 24 (1978):934-948.

6

Strategy Evaluation and Selection

"Money and currency are strange things. They keep on going up and down and no one knows why. If you try to win you lose, no matter how hard you try."
                                        —Abbot Gilles Li Muisis of Tournai

The discussion in this chapter bridges the research and decision phases of the strategic-planning process (see figure 6-1). Strategy evaluation is part of the research done to support the strategic plan; strategy selection, which is often self-evident after all the previous work is completed, is the first decision in the decision phase. First, techniques commonly required during an evaluation to accommodate qualitative issues and missing data are covered. Second, the focus turns to evaluating the strategies in terms of financial goals. Then nonfinancial evaluation criteria are discussed, and finally the selection of the strategy to be implemented is considered.

Evaluation Techniques

Quantifying Qualitative Issues

There are several ways of attempting to quantify qualitative issues; most are similar to the techniques described here. Table 6-1 shows the major steps in the process. The example chosen is a comparison of the marketing and distribution strengths of the planner's company P with those of competitors A and B. The products are assumed to be sold by a direct-sales force to major purchasers and through distributors to small purchasers. In addition, it is assumed that the products are used for medical purposes, so it is important to be aware of federal Food and Drug Administration regulations as well as consumer regulations, product liability problems, and so on.

The first step is to list the major activities performed by the marketing and distribution staff. Next, list the essential elements of each activity. For example, the interface with the regulatory agencies might require one or more people experienced in the operations of regulatory agencies, specific expertise in the agencies of direct interest, legal knowledge, lobbying capability and a sense of public relations, knowledge of the industry (what products is it believed the competition is developing that the regulatory process might delay?), corporate knowledge (what product is your company

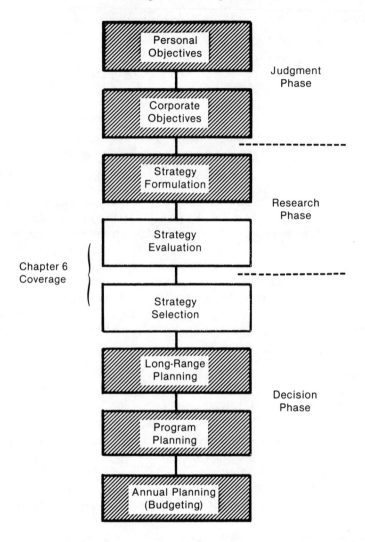

Figure 6-1. The Strategic-Planning Process for Smaller Businesses (Chapter 6 Coverage)

developing that may fall under regulatory control? Can it be avoided?), and other skills. The lists of activities and elements should be as comprehensive as possible and reflect the ideal situation rather than company P's situation to make the comparison with the competition more meaningful. Using the lists, assign weighting factors to each activity. The weights should add up to

Table 6-1

An Example of Quantifying Qualitative Issues: Marketing/Distribution for a Medical Product

| | | Company P | | Competitors | | | |
| | | | | A | | B | |
Activity	Weight	Score	Weighted Score	Score	Weighted Score	Score	Weighted Score
Direct sales	15	2	30	2	30	2	30
Distributor sales	15	3	45	1	15	2	30
Regulatory interface	20	2	40	1	20	0	0
Promotion	10	3	30	2	20	2	20
Market research	10	0	0	1	10	3	30
Brand image	10	1	10	3	30	2	20
Service	10	2	20	1	10	2	20
Customer support	10	1	10	2	20	2	20
Totals	100		185		155		170

100. Justify the weights by discussion with others, examples, and judgment. A significant activity is an accepted area of management interest; if its weight appears to be zero or close to zero, it should be downgraded to the rank of an essential element in another activity. The essential elements should have approximately equal weights. If it appears that one of them deserves greater attention, it should probably be upgraded to a significant activity.

Now score each company in each activity by examining the presence or absence of essential elements (see table 6-2). Reduce the activity scores to the range zero to four: zero means the functions of that activity are essentially absent, while four means that they are present and performed to the highest standards of the industry. The range zero to four allows for three

Table 6-2

An Example of Scoring an Activity: Regulatory Interface

Element	Present/Absent[a]
Experience in agency operations	1
Specific agency experience	0
Legal knowledge	0
Lobbying experience	0
Industry knowledge	1
Company knowledge	1
Technical expertise	1
Total	4 (out of 7)
Adjusted total for range 0 to 4	2.29 ($4 \times 4/7$ = 2.29)

Note: The activity score is rounded down to 2 and entered in table 6-1 under "Score."

[a] 1 means element present; 0 means element absent.

intermediate ratings. The assignment of five rating levels is a realistic assessment of the accuracy that can be achieved with the process since it relies so heavily on personal judgment. A simple interpretation of the rating levels follows.

0 means activity not performed;

1 means activity performed below industry average;

2 means activity performed at industry average;

3 means activity performed above industry average; and

4 means activity performed at the highest standards of the industry.

A further application of the test of realism means that scores of four should be relatively rare. Zero scores ought to be also.

Now multiply the activity scores by their weights and add the results for each company. The highest possible score is 400. Comparing the results provides a good indication of the relative strengths of the competitors. In this example in table 6-2, the planner's company has a marginal advantage over both competitors, but none of them excel in this function. Company P appears to do very little for the customer, which probably explains its poor brand image, but it promotes its products heavily and has excellent distributor sales. Its promotion is probably aimed at distributors and not the end user. Company A, on the other hand, appears to be more oriented to the end user, with better customer support and brand image than company P. Company B performs more market research than companies A or P, but B has no relationship with the relevant regulatory agencies. If B adds competent persons to the staff and lifts the rating in this activity to two or higher, both A and P can expect problems as B's product development benefits from the new data. P can fight back by doing market research and attempting to improve its brand image.

Of course, there are limitations to the process set by the amount of personal judgment required and by the lack of precise data about some of the competitors. But for many business people, performing such an exercise and getting quantitative measures of what was originally a qualitative issue is very helpful. A variation on the presentation of the results is shown in figure 6-2, where the scores are represented by circles shaded from open (a zero score) to solid (a four score). Some visualize the situation better when it is presented this way.

The technique presented here assumes one person will perform the evaluation with occasional discussions with other people. These discussions can be formalized. A group of knowledgeable people can be asked to develop ratings individually. The organizer compares ratings and asks any participant who has one or more ratings markedly different from the

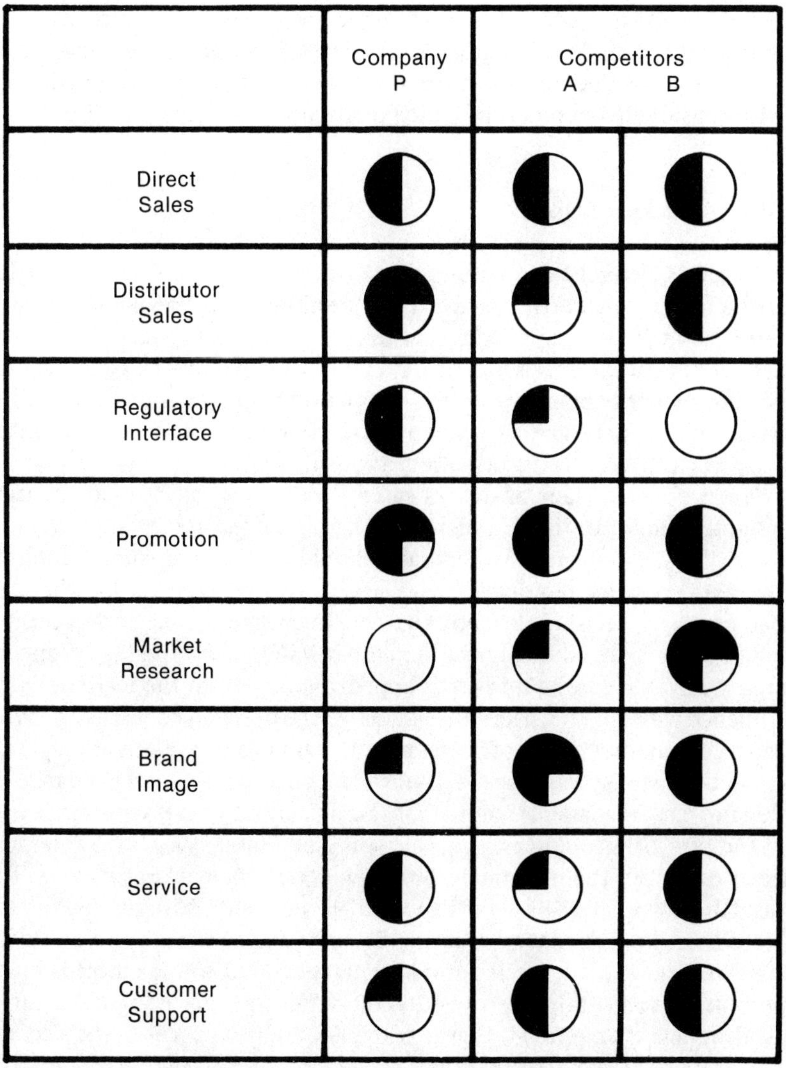

	Company P	Competitors A	B
Direct Sales	◖	◖	◖
Distributor Sales	◕	◔	◖
Regulatory Interface	◖	◔	○
Promotion	◕	◖	◖
Market Research	○	◕	◕
Brand Image	◔	◕	◖
Service	◖	◔	◖
Customer Support	◔	◖	◖

Figure 6-2. Graphical Representation of the Activity Scores Given in Table 6-1

others' for a justification. This process can be repeated several times, providing the participants with the results and justifications from the previous cycles. The information is presented without attribution to an individual. The repetition forces the individuals concerned to think more deeply about their original selections. However, discounting, anchoring, and adjustment (see chapter 3) still occur. When a general consensus has been reached, the task is terminated. This is known as the *Delphi technique*. It is more complicated than the first approach and most small businesses are only likely to use it occasionally to quantify major qualitative issues.

Handling Lack of Data

The Value of Perfect Information. Lack of data is a more difficult problem than handling qualitative issues. The questions "do the data exist anywhere?" and if they do, "what is the cost of obtaining them?" must be asked. In this situation, obtaining data includes expenditures of money and time and may possibly reveal to the competition things about your position such as lack of data and the type of data viewed as important. An astute competitor can use this information to advantage.

The problem of lack of data is eased if decisions can be made by using techniques similar to the ones described here. If none are appropriate, then a search for data outside the company should be made; if some techniques described here work, an outside data search may be avoided, but there is a broad gray area between the two extremes. In every case, the cost of the outside search must be limited to the increase in value of the final decision. The increase in value can be measured approximately from the increase in the confidence with which a decision is made. If the decision concerns an investment to open a new sales office in a new region, and the missing data are good market statistics for the region, then a cost justification similar to the following can be made. Assume that the owner/CEO is 80 percent certain that the new office will generate sales of $250,000 per year, the minimum needed to justify the investment in a new office. A market survey will increase the owner/CEO's confidence to 98 percent. Without the survey, there is a 20-percent chance of losing $20,000 if the office has to be closed. With the survey, the level of confidence is increased so that there is only a 2-percent chance of losing the $20,000. The cost of the market survey should be less than $3,600, that is $20,000 × (20% − 2%)—the decrease in the amount at risk. If the survey costs more than $3,600, the cost of the new data exceeds the increase in the value of the decision.

Using Assumptions. Most techniques used in the absence of data start by assuming values for the missing data, examining the results for credibility and testing the results for sensitivity to changes in the assumptions. If the results are credible and they do not depend in a sensitive manner on the assumptions, then it is reasonable to continue to use the assumptions with the caveat that they should be clearly marked as assumptions, and the final conclusions should have a footnote noting the assumptions. Greater confidence in the process can be established by using a range of assumptions and quoting the results as a range. This shows the sensitivity immediately and the information is carried forward with the analysis rather than in notes.

The Monte Carlo Technique. Greater confidence can be achieved if it is possible to judge the chances that extreme values in the range will occur when compared with the middle values. Then values for the assumed data can be selected at random by using random-number tables and performing the analysis with them. If this is done a large number of times (this requires a computer), the results can be ordered from lowest to highest and information gained about the chances that the result will exceed a given value. This is called the *Monte Carlo* technique. An example is given in figure 6-3, which shows the results of a Monte Carlo analysis to justify the installation of an intraoffice data-communications network linking data terminals to each other and to computers. The missing data here include the cost-benefit per terminal to be derived from the installation of the network, and financial parameters such as fluctuations in inflation rates and interest rates. A range of values for each missing value was assumed and a random-number generator used to select values for use in the calculation of the net present value (present worth) of the investment. The calculations were performed on a personal computer. They showed a 50-percent chance that the payback period would be less than three years and a 50-percent chance that it would exceed three years. The time periods for payback associated with 10-percent, 30-percent, 70-percent, and 90-percent chances were also provided.

Discussion

Although these techniques do provide a way of continuing with an analysis in the absence of data, they do not eliminate the need for data. Also, the techniques that yield probabilities do not establish absolute probabilities, but relative probabilities in a range determined by the assumptions. If the range is wrong, the results are wrong. In the intraoffice-data-terminal example, a sensitivity calculation was performed to determine how sensitive the results would be to frequent reconfiguration of the communications network as people changed offices; the result was that the payback period was relatively insensitive to these moves if less than 25 percent of the terminals were moved per year. This result has a much greater chance of validity than an attempt to determine absolutely the payback period, since it does not depend on establishing the true values of the cost-benefit, inflation rate, or interest rate.

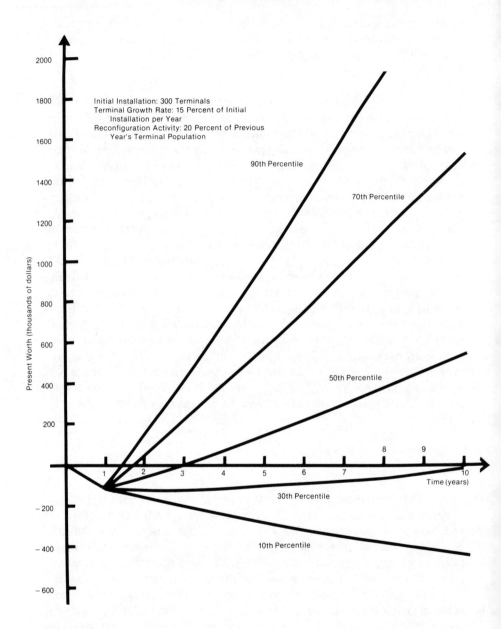

Figure 6-3. An Example of a Monte Carlo Calculation: The Present Worth of an Investment in an Intraoffice Communications Network

Financial Evaluation Criteria

The ultimate test for any business is its ability to operate with an acceptable profit. The established ways of evaluating this are the profit-and-loss statement and the balance sheet. However, these financial statements rely on numerous assumptions and usually need to be analyzed with other data in order to develop a proper picture of the state of the business. Part of the evaluation of the alternative strategic plans is to prepare pro-forma profit-and-loss statements and balance sheets. If they do not demonstrate the achievement of a profit large enough to provide a satisfactory return on the shareholders' equity as measured by the balance sheet, then the strategy needs to be reconsidered. Unfortunately, this evaluation may not be a stringent-enough test of the strategy for small businesses and should not be the first financial test made.

Most small businesses need a more stringent test of the viability of a strategic plan than the pro-forma accounts. Certainly they measure financial strength in a standardized manner. But they only determine this strength at annual intervals associated with the passage of time, not at intervals associated with the implementation of the strategic plan, which would be a more natural measure. A small business needs financial tests that measure the operating capability of the business on a continuing basis so that the impact of the strategic plan on the operations can be measured. The most satisfactory measure for this is cash flow supported by an analysis of sources and applications of funds.

The Time Value of Money

Most analytical texts on business finances emphasize the time value of money: one dollar earned today is worth more than one dollar earned a year from today because the dollar earned today can be invested and can earn interest. Similarly, if it is known that a payment must be made one year from now, it is only necessary to put aside a lesser amount so that it earns interest for the year and reaches the amount required for the payment. Deferring a payment until tomorrow is valuable. The interest rate used to relate the value of receipts and payments at different times is called the *discount rate*, and calculations of the cash flow needed to operate a business over a period of years are called *discounted cash-flow analyses* when a discount rate is used to state the receipts and payments in terms of the value of money in one year, usually the first year of the calculation, when it is called the *present worth* or *present value* of future cash transactions. Table 6-3 shows a simple example of such a calculation.

There are several ways to analyze discounted cash-flow data: to determine net present value, internal rate of return, and payback period. The net

Table 6-3
An Example of a Net-Present-Value Calculation

Year	Item	Cash Flow (dollars)	Discount Factor	Discounted Cash Flow (dollars)
1	Purchase price	−90,000	1.00	−90,000
1	Installation costs	−4,000	1.00	−4,000
1	Increased margin	+13,500	1.00	+13,500
1	Sale of old machine	+3,000	1.00	+3,000
2	Increased margin	+18,000	1.10	+16,364
3	Increased margin	+18,000	1.21	+14,876
4	Increased margin	+18,000	1.331	+13,524
5	Overhaul cost	−9,000	1.4641	−6,147
5	Increased margin	+16,500	1.4641	+11,270
6	Increased margin	+18,000	1.6105	+11,177
7	Increased margin	+18,000	1.7716	+10,160
8	Increased margin	+18,000	1.9487	+9,237
9	Salvage value	+9,000	2.1436	+4,199
Net present value				+7,160

Note: In this example a company wishes to replace some manufacturing equipment. The purchase price is $90,000; the installation costs $4,000 and takes one month. The projected improvement in productivity over the old machine leads to increased margins of $500 per month for months 2, 3, and 4, and $1,500 per month for every month thereafter. The old machine is sold for $3,000 during the first year. The new machine will require a major overhaul after four years, costing $9,000 and requiring a one-month interruption in production. The projected salvage value after eight years of use is $9,000. The discount rate used by the company is 10 percent per year. Is the investment justified? The net present value based on the assumptions and data given here is +$7,160; thus the investment is justified.

present value of an investment is the difference between the present value of all the receipts made over the years of the analysis and the present value of all the payments made over the years. If the present value is positive, then the investment is producing a return; if the present value is negative, then the investment is losing money. In figure 6-3, the present value is plotted against the number of years considered. The value at one year represents the present value assuming the investment only has a life of one year. As can be seen, this value is negative in all cases in this example since one year is too short a time for the investment to start to generate income. By ten years, the present value is positive since the investment has had time to earn income. The year in which the present value turns from negative to positive represents the year in which the payback of the investment starts and is commonly called the *payback period*. The internal-rate-of-return calculation is an inverted discounted cash-flow calculation since it seeks to evaluate the discount rate—internal rate of return—required to generate zero present value given the investment, operating costs, and revenues.

Different companies place different weights on the analysis methods discussed. Many only invest in programs that provide an internal rate of return above a certain level. Others use the net-present-value calculations to select between alternative programs (the one with the highest value being the best) and then determine whether the selected program is good enough to meet the internal-rate-of-return criterion. Most companies also look at the payback period since too long a period implies greater risk and a longer time that they must continue to invest in the program before seeing a return.

The Direct Cash-Flow Test

None of the techniques discussed so far appear to address the real problem of small businesses, namely, how much cash is required before the program starts to recover cash faster than it is being expended. Table 6-4 gives an example of a direct cash-flow calculation. Too frequently, the extreme negative excursion in cash flow is beyond the capabilities of a small business. This problem is compounded by the fact that not all the cash in a sequence of transactions flows quickly. The discounted cash-flow techniques usually concentrate on time periods divided into yearly increments. Even within one year, there can be remarkable differences in cash flow for a company. A toy store, making purchases in the early fall for sales made near Christmas and paid for by check and credit card, faces at least a four-month wait between expenditures and receipts. Yet expenditures and receipts occur in the same year if accrual accounting is used and probably would be accounted for in the same year using a discounted cash-flow calculation. The same thing occurs to the manufacturing company that buys parts for assembly into products which are sold later, as illustrated earlier in figure 5-4. All these elements stand in the way of prompt cash flow. The discounted cash-flow technique uses too coarse a time scale for most small businesses.

The recommended evaluation approach for small businesses is to perform a direct cash-flow calculation, evaluating expenses and revenues for shorter time intervals than one year (three months at most and one month if possible) to determine the maximum negative cash flow involved. The cash flows for each time interval should be added together and the magnitude of the extreme negative cash flow for that plan compared with the company's ability to support it.

In table 6-4, the investment easily passed the discounted cash-flow test based on the life of the equipment, but by the twenty-fifth month of ownership, the business has to find $67,080 in cash to cover the costs involved in acquiring, installing, and operating the equipment; this is after the extra margins generated by the equipment are taken into account. In fact, the cash-flow situation will gradually get worse until the loan is repaid.

Table 6-4
An Example of a Direct Cash-Flow Calculation

Month	Item	Cash Flow (dollars)	Cumulative Cash Flow (dollars)
1	Purchase price	− 90,000	− 90,000
1	Installation costs	− 4,000	− 94,000
1	Loan	+ 60,000	− 34,000
1	Compensating balance	− 6,000	− 40,000
2	Extra materials	− 500	− 40,500
3	Extra materials	− 500	− 41,000
4	Extra materials	− 500	− 41,500
5	Extra materials	− 500	− 42,000
6	Extra materials	− 500	− 42,500
7	Extra materials	− 500	− 43,000
7	Increased margin	+ 500	− 42,500
7	Cost of removing old machine	− 2,000	− 44,500
8	Extra materials	− 500	− 45,000
8	Increased margin	+ 500	− 44,500
9	Extra materials	− 500	− 45,000
9	Increased margin	+ 500	− 44,500
9	Proceeds of sale of old machine	+ 3,000	− 41,500
10	Extra materials	− 500	− 42,000
10	Increased margin	+ 1,500	− 40,500
11	Extra materials	− 500	− 41,000
11	Increased margin	+ 1,500	− 39,500
12	Extra materials	− 500	− 40,000
12	Increased margin	+ 1,500	− 38,500
13	Extra materials	− 500	− 39,000
13	Loan principal repayment	− 12,000	− 51,000
13	Loan interest repayment	− 9,600	− 60,600
13	Reduced compensating balance	+ 1,200	− 59,400
13	Increased margin	+ 1,500	− 57,900

* * *

Month	Item	Cash Flow (dollars)	Cumulative Cash Flow (dollars)
24	Extra materials	− 500	− 48,400
24	Increased margin	+ 1,500	− 46,900
25	Increased materials	− 500	− 47,400
25	Loan principal repayment	− 12,000	− 59,400
25	Loan interest repayment	− 7,680	− 67,080
25	Reduced compensating balance	+ 1,200	− 65,880
25	Increased margin	+ 1,500	− 64,380

Note: The company borrows two-thirds of the purchase price for the equipment referred to in table 6-3. The loan is for five years at an interest rate of 16 percent per year with annual repayments of $12,000 plus interest on the balance outstanding. The bank also requires a compensating balance equal to 10 percent of the outstanding loan principal. The improved productivity of the machine requires the purchase of additional raw materials at a cost of $500 per month over the previous purchases; it is assumed that they are paid for on delivery. The production goes into work in progress, finished-goods inventory, and accounts receivable so the increased margin of $1,500 per month is not realized until five months after production. The old machine costs $2,000 to remove. It is sold for cash in the ninth month.

The discounted cash-flow calculation can be done on the same detailed basis but unless the results are examined, the size of the cash outflow is hidden. Neither example presented here includes the impact of taxation on the cash flow. This should be considered in a full evaluation.

Break-even Analysis

The cash-flow test cannot be performed in isolation. It is helpful to determine how the size of the business activity affects the finances of the company, and to determine whether the rate of return from the activity is acceptable. The usual approach to the first issue is to perform a break-even calculation. Figure 6-4 and table 6-5 present results of a typical calculation. The break-even point is calculated as the point at which revenues equal the total of the fixed and variable costs. The fixed costs are those associated with factors normally regarded as not changing when the volume of production changes, while the variable costs change directly with the number of units manufactured.

Even though the program to manufacture and sell this particular product appears very attractive, it is important to relate this type of calculation to the absolute cash-flow situation. The first reaction on looking at the results of figure 6-4 and table 6-5 is to increase production as quickly as possible. Even if you are sure that the market is available, this is not necessarily the best thing to do. More production means buying more materials and components, paying more wages, paying more for shipping costs, and perhaps requiring more warehouse space. It also means increasing parts, work-in-progress and finished-goods inventories, and issuing more invoices that increase the accounts receivable. Unfortunately, neither the fixed nor variable costs are constants, especially in rapid-growth situations. A new clerk may be required to handle the extra purchase orders, production scheduling, and invoicing. The insurance charges may increase. A new delivery vehicle may be required. A second shift adds to the utilities bill. And so on. These items traditionally have been regarded as fixed costs as production increases. The variable costs also increase as new production workers are hired who are less productive until trained, more quality control is required, and so on.

One counterforce is the possibility of receiving price discounts from suppliers for increased purchases of parts and materials, but this advantage has to be balanced against increases in inventory that utilize cash. In order to encourage sales of the new product, discounts to customers and additional bonuses to sales personnel may be offered that reduce the average selling price and increase the sales costs. All these phenomena tend to increase the volume of production needed to break even. They also affect cash flow severely as inventories and accounts receivable increase.

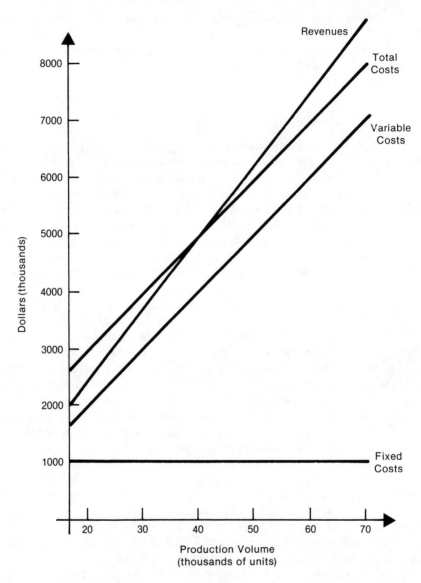

Figure 6-4. An Example of a Break-even Calculation Using Direct Costing

The break-even technique is useful for setting production volumes and prices needed to achieve a certain level of profitability or a break-even point, which is zero profits. The example given here uses the direct-costing method, which treats all fixed costs as expenses in the period of interest.

Table 6-5
An Example of a Break-even Calculation Using Direct Costing

Production Volume (thousands of units)	Revenues (thousands (of dollars)	Variable Costs (thousands of dollars)	Fixed Costs (thousands of dollars)	Total Costs (thousands of dollars)
20	2,500	2,000	1,000	3,000
30	3,750	3,000	1,000	4,000
40	5,000	4,000	1,000	5,000
50	6,250	5,000	1,000	6,000
60	7,500	6,000	1,000	7,000
70	8,750	7,000	1,000	8,000

Note: Unit sales price is $125. Variable cost per unit manufactured is $100. Break-even occurs at a production volume of 40,000 units.

An alternative approach that is widely used is the absorption-costing method in which the fixed manufacturing costs are assigned to an overhead factor based on the standard production expected for the year. If the fixed costs are $250,000 for the year and the standard production is 25,000 units, then the overhead for each unit manufactured is $10. Detailed calculations not included here show that the break-even volume is less when calculated using the absorption-costing technique. This is because the value of the inventory is now increased by the overhead attributed to each item in inventory.

Grossman, Plum, and Welker describe the two approaches in more detail. They also demonstrate the power of the break-even method as a managerial tool when the fixed costs are divided into fixed manufacturing costs, fixed selling costs, and fixed administration costs, and the variable costs are divided into manufacturing, selling, and administration costs. Costs are also divided into classes depending on whether the variable-cost element depends on production volume or on the product price (sales commissions vary with volume and price for example).[1]

Strategies calling for growth need to be reviewed carefully to determine when the break-even point will occur and how growth will affect the cash flow. The conservative approach is to assume that all payments are made the day the goods or services are ordered while all receipts are delayed for sixty days after the invoices are issued. In tight economic conditions, the sixty-day period may be low. For very small businesses, the assumption of cash payments for all purchases is probably true.

Return on Investment

The calculation of return on investment made in a new program can be deceiving in a small business and lead to day-to-day operational problems even when the return looks attractive. The problem is that calculating the profit does not take into account the cash flow. Management decisions made to increase profitability and return can actually stress cash flow further. Once again, the issue is that establishing a figure for profit requires the establishment of an operating time period over which to measure the profit without examining the fluctuations in cash flow that occur on a daily basis during the period.

After the profit is calculated, establishing the return on investment requires calculating the current level of investment in the business. Just calculating the amount of the investment is open to discussion since several techniques are possible.[2] One method is to add the totals of the original investment, any later investments, and the retained earnings from the operation of the business. This excludes depreciation allowances on property bought with the invested funds; the allowances reduce the investment figure. Small businesses, in order to derive the return on a particular program, should compare the profit from that program with the incremental investment made to support it. Rather than try to compare this return with rates of return in other industries or investments in securities or money-market funds, compare it with standard rates of return in the industry you operate in, and with the usual rate of return earned by your business.

Strategic plans that reduce the business's usual rate of return should be reconsidered. Using industry- and business-specific rates as a standard of comparison avoids many of the problems—usually tinged with regret—that can occur when making comparisons with outside activities of a different nature. If the personal-planning activities described in chapter 3 were performed thoroughly, the owner/CEO is in an appropriate business and comparisons are better made within that framework. If the strategic-planning exercise reveals that the business cannot satisfy the owner/CEO's personal objectives, then a very difficult decision is required to determine whether to change businesses and how to do so.

Sustainable Growth Rate

Aggressive growth plans usually require borrowing money and establishing credit lines as well as increased equity investment. A simple formula has been developed for use by planners to measure the capability of a business to grow. It is:

$$G = P[R + (D/E) \times (R - I)],$$

where

G is the sustainable growth rate in percentage per year,

P is the percentage of earnings retained,

R is the return on net assets expressed as a percentage,

D/E is the debt-to-equity ratio, and

I is the effective interest rate on the debt after allowing for income tax, expressed as a percentage.

The equation contains two terms, the sustainable growth rate from retained earnings alone, and the sustainable growth rate from borrowing. Both retained earnings and the borrowing can be regarded as increases in the company's net assets, and the amount of extra money they create to invest in further growth is readily calculated by multiplying the increase in net assets by the average return on net assets achieved by the company. However, part of the return has to be used to repay the interest on the loan so the return on the loan has to be reduced by the effective interest cost. The effective interest cost takes into account the reduction in taxable income allowed by Internal Revenue Service regulations.

Although this equation gives a general estimation of growth rates, shown in table 6-6, it should be used with caution. Lenders will look very carefully at what the business's debt-to-equity ratio will be after the loan is received. Many rules of thumb have been quoted for an acceptable ratio but it will depend critically on local circumstances in the business including the length of time it has been operating. Also, the equation makes no allowance for repayment of principal, which has to come out of retained earnings. Clearly, it makes no sense to borrow to secure growth if the return on assets is less than the true interest rate. Further caution is required if existing debt is supporting growth programs initiated in previous years. It is probably better to use the ratio of the extra debt to be incurred for the strategic plan under consideration to the incremental equity available for the program to calculate the program's sustainable growth rate rather than the absolute ratio between total debt and total equity. This will give a better indication of

Table 6-6
Sustainable Corporate Growth Rates

Financial Parameters	Sustainable Growth Rate (percentage per annum)			
Debt to equity ratio	0.5	1.0	1.5	2.0
Retained earnings (percentage)				
50	6.88	7.75	8.63	9.50
75	10.31	11.63	12.94	14.25
100	13.75	15.50	17.25	19.00

Note: Return on assets is assumed to be 12.0 percent. The effective interest rate on debt is assumed to be 8.5 percent.

the growth rate resulting from that strategy plan. The value of the debt-to-equity ratio used in the equation may exceed the usual value with less fear of losing the loan since banks will look at the absolute ratio in coming to their decisions. One problem is that this equation still does not take cash flow into consideration. A strategy may have an attractive growth rate and still plunge the business into financial difficulties.

Judging the correct growth rate for assets, especially for production equipment and facilities, is difficult. The tendency is to plan to match productive capacity to projected sales quite closely. Precise matching is impossible because sales grow in small increments while productive capacity usually grows in major increments. However, the greatest return is not necessarily from 100-percent utilization of a facility. Spare capacity is often desirable for scheduling flexibility and to ease incremental changes in product design or process technology. A poor mix of machines may negatively affect overall efficiency of production even if they are fully utilized. Also, there are hidden costs associated with old machines that need more frequent maintenance and with new machines that demand better, more costly raw materials and more sophisticated maintenance.

Another way to look at growth and its impact on the operations of the company is to monitor changes in orders in relation to production capacity and shipments.[3] For the purposes of this evaluation, issuing invoices (billing) is a good measure of shipments, and the ratio of orders booked to shipping is called the book-to-bill ratio. If bookings are increasing faster than billings, then the business is growing. Unfortunately, the growth will appear as lengthened backlogs and eventually as lost orders if the orders exceed the production capacity on a regular basis. The chart shown in table 6-7 shows the results of calculations relating the backlog duration to increasing bookings and the growth in the business. Information of this type helps the planner examine the needs for new capacity, gauge the impact of limits on the company's ability to add new capacity, and provides a good management tool to monitor growth on a monthly basis.

Table 6-7
Annual Growth in Revenues Consistent with Constant Backlog and Constant Book-to-Bill Ratio

Ratio/Duration	Growth Rate in Revenues (percentage per annum)		
Book-to-bill ratio	1.05	1.10	1.15
Backlog duration (months)			
2	35.5	85.1	154.9
4	16.3	35.5	58.2
6	10.6	22.3	35.5

The Impact of Inflation

Detailed cash-flow analyses frequently involve allowances for inflation. The importance of inflation in managing a small business depends on the business's time horizons, the length of the production cycle, and its general impact on the cost of materials, components, capital equipment, services, labor, and interest rates.

Concentrating on cash flow on a month-to-month basis is the recommended approach for evaluating strategic plans and usually this time horizon is shorter than the period in which major impacts from inflation occur. The real issue in this cash-flow orientation is the ability to raise prices as inflation pressures take their toll on costs. If competitive pressures make this difficult to achieve, then a more sophisticated evaluation technique using a second discount factor to bring all the dollar flows to constant dollars is probably required. Otherwise, performing the cash-flow analysis in current dollars without attention to inflation is adequate, at least for one or two years in periods of moderate inflation.

Inflation will start to affect the profit-and-loss statement and the balance sheet as time passes. In particular, the question of depreciating fixed assets from a value established by their purchase costs is a concern. In practice, replacing the asset will cost more as a result of inflationary pressures and the depreciation allowances are too small as a result. Theoretically, ignoring inflation while evaluating strategic alternatives is acceptable if the alternatives are similar and they do not involve analyses over lengthy time periods. The recommended evaluation technique is based on the need to maintain operating strength in the business. Every year the business's performance must be measured by the profit-and-loss statement and balance sheet, and every year the strategic-planning process must consider the performance of the business in beating inflation and providing for replacement of assets, not just in growth.

Sources of Funds

A cash-flow analysis of one strategic alternative does not necessarily consider the interplay of the sources and applications of funds in the business. If a large negative cash flow is revealed, then the owner/CEO must consider whether this can be supported and how. The sustainable growth-rate calculation showed the leverage to be gained from loans as long as a lender can be found and the principal payments are covered by the cash flow. More often than not, the owner/CEO will have to seek sources of funds for the programs within the business. This requires an analysis of the total business cash flow to determine whether other sources, not specifically included in the strategic option under consideration, can provide funds in a timely manner. If they can, by definition they are now part of the strategic alternative. An example would be the sale of a building or land no longer needed by the business. The funds can be applied to support the most attractive strategies and absorb larger negative cash flows than would otherwise be possible. If this route is chosen, then disposing of the property would become a key part of the strategy.

A more sophisticated example involves the use of profits from an established product line to fund the development of a new product line. While the first considerations of the strategy covered the identification of the new product line to take advantage of corporate strengths, market opportunities, and competitors' weaknesses, now the funding issue also involves the future of the existing product line. In large businesses, two product lines may be sufficiently distinct that they can be the subject of separate strategies; in small businesses this separation is unlikely. The evaluation of the different strategy options is now the evaluation of the business operations assuming each strategy in turn is in place. As a simplification, it is reasonable to start by considering each strategy as an increment to the business and look at the costs and benefits of the increment using the cash-flow test. If a strategy passes that test, the next stage is to look at the cash flow for the total business including the strategy. This forces the identification of the sources and applications of funds and draws attention to the strategic significance to the business of actions that might otherwise have been regarded as normal.

Pro-Forma Financial Statements

The final part of the evaluation is to develop pro-forma financial statements, in particular the profit-and-loss statement and the balance sheet. These support the strategy-evaluation process, and are the accepted means of monitoring a business's performance over a period of years. They do not provide as stringent a test of a company's ability to operate the strategy as the cash-flow test does.

Many small businesses, in order to reduce costs and minimize time spent on accounting, use a statement of earnings and expenses prepared for the federal income-tax authorities as the profit-and-loss statement, and prepare their balance sheet using the same figures. Using tax accounts may be inappropriate. There is significant incentive to decrease income and increase operating expenses in order to minimize the tax obligation; while the more desirable approach for a business is to increase revenues and minimize expenses. Also, the depreciation tables allowed by the Internal Revenue Service do not necessarily measure the true economic life of the capital equipment for the user, nor reserve the right amount of money to replace it at the end of its useful life. Maintaining two sets of accounts, one that reflects the cost of doing business using assumptions tailored to the industry concerned, and one that adheres to Internal Revenue Service guidelines, is advisable.

Nonfinancial Evaluation Criteria

There are four major nonfinancial evaluation criteria to use in evaluating the alternative strategic plans. They are

1. the existence of viable contingency plans;
2. the extent to which the plan depends on assumptions;
3. the clear distinction between avoidable and unavoidable risks; and
4. the clear distinction between acceptable and unacceptable risks.

Contingency Plans

Numerous assumptions have been made during the development of the strategic plans. The major assumptions must be identified and examined in more detail to determine what courses of action are available if one or more of them proves to be incorrect. These courses of action must be contained in contingency plans associated with the main strategies.

If a business plans to open a sales office in another region as growth renews after a recession, the contingency plans are relatively straightforward; if the recession does not abate as quickly as forecast, then implementing the expansion plans is delayed. In particular, major capital investments in the new area are delayed until there are clear signs that the economy is recovering. A more complex example occurs if a new product or service fails to generate sales as quickly as expected. This is not an unusual situation but the question is "why?"

Several variations of a contingency plan are required to accommodate several possible circumstances. The problem is to determine which combination of circumstances has contributed to the missed sales targets so that the correct contingency plan can be implemented. Perhaps the product is priced too high. If this is true, can price adjustments be made without endangering the cash flow? Perhaps the customers' needs were not adequately analyzed. If so, what is the cost of performing a better analysis and correcting the mistake? Can the cash flow absorb this cost? Will the delay make the product obsolete or allow the competition to gain a significant advantage? Are there reliability and field-service problems that are frightening potential customers away? Once again, how much will it cost and how long will it take to correct these? Is it simply that the customer is unaware of the product and the manufacturer? Will an enlarged advertising campaign help?

The contingency plans should contain estimates of price changes that can be made without too much difficulty and estimates of the cost and timing to improve the product or its marketing if necessary. If everything goes well, these product-improvement programs may be called on to take advantage of a major expansion in the market rather than to combat a poor market.

The ultimate contingency plan is to stop the activity entirely. If this occurs, the strategy-planning process that led to the selection of that activity should be reviewed carefully to derive guidance for improving the process the next time. In practice, the next time starts with the decision to stop the activity since that is a strategic decision of some magnitude. However, survival of the business is the most important element. Without the business there is no need for a strategic plan, and no business vehicle by which personal goals can be met.

Evaluating Assumptions

The strategic plans contain a number of assumptions, both explicit and tacit. Some of them may include changes in environmental factors. The planner should evaluate the plans to see which assumptions are under his control, which are under his influence, and which are completely independent. If there are too many assumptions about factors beyond the planner's influence, the plan is suspect. In that case, examine the range of assumptions. What is the worst outcome of the assumption? The most likely? The best? Does it matter? Is the plan still viable under the worst-case assumption? If so, even though it is beyond the planner's control or influence, the plan passes that test. It is a sound precaution to perform the same test on the assumptions within the planner's control or influence.

Table 6-8 gives a simplified example of how the process can be summarized. Note the two items at the bottom of the table: one lists the assumptions in terms of positive and negative impacts on the plan; the other lists indicators to monitor to determine whether the assumptions are still correct, or for assumptions concerning events yet to occur. These items help the planner make the original evaluation, and, if the plan is adopted, maintain the evaluation.

Classification of Risks

The classification of risks into avoidable and unavoidable risks was discussed in chapters 3 and 5. The strategic plan should not contain any avoidable risks

Table 6-8
An Example of Evaluating Assumptions

	Outcome		
Assumption	*Worst*	*Most Likely*	*Best*
Under own control			
Increased productivity	0%	+3%	+7%
Major new product introduction	In 15th month	In 8th month	In 6th month
Under own influence			
Patent protection for new product	No	Yes, with changes to claims	Yes, as is
First-year sales of new product	$1 million	$3 million	$4 million
Not under own control or influence			
Inflation in costs	+12%	+8%	+6%
Competitor introduces better product	Yes	Yes, but suffers some early problems	Yes, but market slow to accept it

* * *

Positive impact	New product; patent; productivity improvement.
Negative impact	Inflation; competitor's new product.
Indicators to monitor for	
Increased productivity	Reduced variable costs
New-product introduction	Successful evaluation of prototype; successful field test of several prototypes.
Patent protection	Office actions.
First-year sales	Enquiry rate; order rate.
Inflation	Monthly government statistics.
Competitor's product	Trade press; trade show; comments from prospective customers

and it must clearly identify unavoidable risks, dividing them into acceptable and unacceptable risks. The strategic plan should not contain any unacceptable risks. The owner/CEO will eventually have to make these risk evaluations alone. They relate closely to the self-appraisal of risk tendencies. Also, it is not often possible to gain agreement on risks because of the highly personal nature of risk tendencies. If the executives and senior managers think that the owner/CEO is taking unreasonable risks, the owner/CEO will have to be firm in stating that the risks do not appear unreasonable. Nevertheless, the staff's comments should be listened to carefully and objectively before making the final decision. This is the class of decision that distinguishes the owner/CEO from the staff and justifies the rewards received by the owner/CEO when the decisions are correct.

Recording the Results

At the end of the evaluation process there should be one strategy for the business that has survived all the tests. If no strategy survives, the evaluation process will have provided important insights into the weaknesses of the candidate strategies, which will help develop more strategies. If the weaknesses of the strategies were all fundamental, a more detailed examination of the major steps in the process using the notes made at each step is called for. Perhaps too optimistic an appraisal of corporate strengths was made; more likely the corporate objectives were too aggressively set, for example, seeking sustained high growth when the borrowing power and cash resources were not available to support it.

If one strategy survives, record the results of the evaluation process in brief notes but do not eliminate the others yet. The task of selecting the strategy is not yet finished.

Strategy Selection

The strategic-planning technique described here establishes major objectives and decision criteria at the very beginning of the process and then, through a series of intermediate steps, collects data and information and performs analyses to develop the plan that best meets the decision criteria and satisfies the major objectives. Each step takes the objectives and decision criteria from the previous steps and specializes them for the current and succeeding steps as the planning process becomes more detailed.

Having evaluated the proposed strategies against stringent business-operating criteria, especially the cash-flow test, it is now necessary to go back to the beginning of the process and determine whether the best strategy still meets the original criteria. The compatible personal and corporate objectives provide a rigorous set of quantitative and qualitative evaluation criteria and the best strategy must survive comparison with them before adoption. It is unlikely to be a perfect match. The strategy may not satisfy the personal objectives in some way or it may not be adequate to ensure the long-term survival of the business. If the areas of deviation are small, it is probably wise to go ahead with the strategy and try to improve the match during the next planning cycle. This is usually possible without any penalty.

Failure to pass this last review requires modifications to the strategy, to the objectives, or to both. All the strategies on the short list are made viable candidates again by the failure of the best. The strategy that failed the last test was selected because it received the highest marks in the evaluation procedure. The others may have had good or acceptable marks and even if they did not, they might still be modified to pass the tests. An analysis of the reasons why each proposal failed may lead to constructive modifications and revitalization of a different strategy. In some cases a combined strategy may be appropriate. More likely, a simplified strategy may be better. A one-dimensional strategy rather than a two-dimensional or three-dimensional strategy may have a better chance of meeting the original objectives. Unfortunately, much work must at least be revised and perhaps even repeated if this occurs, but the benefit is a rigorously tested strategy that, when successful, will meet the objectives. The surviving strategy can now be reduced to detailed plans as described in the next chapter.

Notes

1. Steven D. Grossman, Charles W. Plum, and Robert S. Welker, "New Dimensions to the Cost-Volume-Profit (Breakeven) Technique," *Managerial Planning* 27 (1979):35-38.

2. Leopold A. Bernstein, *The Analysis of Financial Statements*, (Homewood, Ill.: Dow-Jones Irwin, 1978), pp. 147-171.

3. W.F. Arnold, "Chart Refines Book-to-Bill Ratio to Measure Demand versus Capacity," *Electronic Business* 8 (November 1980):112-113.

7 Planning

"With organization and time is found the secret to doing all and doing well."   —Pythagoras

This chapter outlines the planning process needed to implement the selected strategy. This is the decision stage of the strategic-planning process, shown in figure 7-1. The preparation of the minimum set of plans consistent with proper implementation of the strategy and good mangement control is the objective of this phase. Restricting the number and variety of plans helps relieve some of the time pressures felt by executives and managers in small businesses.

Planning involves two major activities: making decisions now that will influence the future course of the business, and preparing for future decisions to be made during the course of business operations. There is a third valuable use of planning, certainly of the long-range plan, that is, communicating the objectives, policies, and programs of the company to the staff.

Planning, at least at the level of budgeting, is widely utilized and well understood. Therefore, the emphasis in this chapter is on linking the plans to the earlier steps in the strategic-planning process and to the control of corporate operations.

The three classes of plans described here are:

1. the long-range plan;
2. program plans; and
3. the annual plan (budget).

Each has a specific role to play and together they cover all the operations of the company. The major differences among them are time coverage and the local set of objectives. Figure 7-2 shows how the plans differ in time coverage. The long-range plan covers the complete time horizon of the company. The program plans differ considerably in length, since several are needed to implement the long-range plan. Preparing a justification for a major capital investment, which may only require a few weeks, is a legitimate subject of a program plan, as are the continuing operations of the training department over a period of years. The annual plan incorporates the program plans into a single, financially-oriented plan for management control of the business for one year. The annual plan is prepared before the

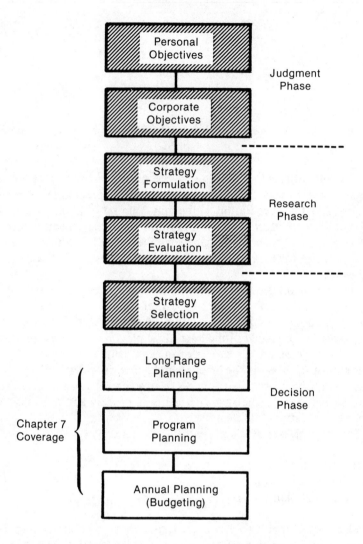

Figure 7-1. The Strategic-Planning Process for Smaller Businesses (Chapter 7 Coverage)

start of the year to which it refers. It should be reviewed at least quarterly and every time a major change in circumstances such as the loss of a major customer or the failure to meet a major goal occurs. Later, reviewing the actual performance against the plan is an important part of the situation analysis for the next strategic plan.

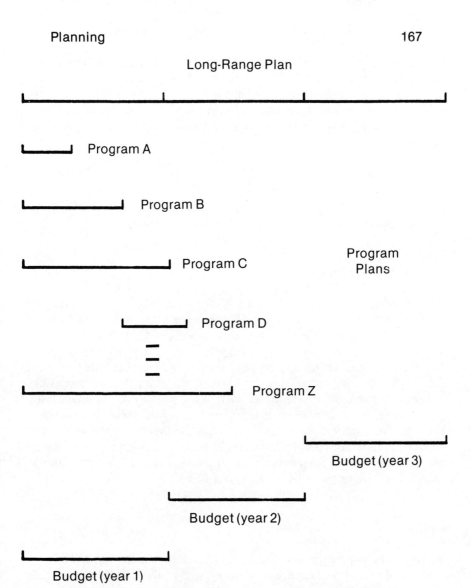

Figure 7-2. The Time Horizons of Different Plans

Preparing Plans

Plan to Plan

It is helpful to plan to plan. The different plans should be assigned to the most appropriate staff members, who should be given directions concerning the objectives to be achieved and the budgetary constraints. The review and revision procedures should be described, time limits for the various steps set, and a plan format established that facilitates integrating the financial outputs from each plan into the basic financial statements used for guidance and control of the business. These basic financial statements include:

the profit-and-loss statement;

the balance sheet;

the statement of sources and applications of funds;

the cash-flow forecast; and

the capital budget.

The owner/CEO has the results of the strategic-planning process including data on the company and its operations, the environment and its likely changes, and competitors and their possible future actions. The people charged with the task of producing the operating plans need access to this information, so the appropriate data should be distributed to those responsible for preparing different parts of the plan. As far as possible, ranges or limits should be given for each numerical forecast or quantitative goal. Ranges are a more realistic representation of the accuracy with which these factors can be defined, and providing planners with absolute values tends to limit their ability to innovate. In the worst case, they feel that the planning has already been done for them and that they are in a clerical role, merely preparing the document in a neat format.

Problems

Planning is an important part of the management process, not a task to be performed when time is available. However, even those companies that do prepare plans regularly can have a problem maintaining the importance of such plans in the minds of the people involved. Attempts must be made to avoid planning becoming a management ritual, when the planners are more concerned that the owner/CEO receives six pages of budget data as requested than they are with the contents of the budget, or with the figures' relationship to their activities over the next few months. Although there are undoubtedly real limits to the financial resources available in the great majority of businesses, it is best to approach planning as an exercise in seeking opportunities rather than an exercise in limiting resources. This fosters a positive attitude toward the process and stimulates exploration of alternative approaches.

Good planning often raises concerns among the planners. It is an introspective and discomforting process. It may shine the harsh light of reality on many activities that have not been reviewed for some time. It can raise doubts in an individual about his or her role in and ability to contribute to the company. These issues are all the more disconcerting given the tendency of individuals to be their own harshest critics. Again, formatting the planning process as a positive exercise, selecting between alternatives, and asking "what if . . . ?" questions helps allay fears that there may be some arbitrary right way that has somehow escaped the planner's attention, and that the failure to find it will cost much effort or even the planner's job.

Long-Range Planning

The long-range plan should be a short document stating:

1. the description of the company's business;
2. the company's business objectives;
3. the resources needed to achieve the objectives;
4. the strategies to be used to achieve the objectives; and
5. the major programs needed to implement the strategies.

The owner/CEO is the most appropriate person to prepare the long-range plan although it can be done by any senior person in the company under the owner/CEO's guidance. The time period to be included should be defined after considering the timing issues discussed in chapter 5. For most small businesses, a two- or three-year period is appropriate, but there can be deviations from this, especially for businesses in the capital-equipment industry that usually need a longer long-range plan. In all cases, it is helpful to include a short section discussing in qualitative terms the years after the period considered in detail.

The description of the company's business is available from the strategic-planning work described in chapter 5. If, as is likely, the small business is treated as one strategic business unit, the definition of the strategic unit should also be summarized. The statement of the company's objectives is available from the work described in chapter 3. Objectives include strategic and financial goals, the latter related to the standard financial statements describing the company's performance.

The list of resources (finances, personnel, facilities, equipment, and technology) has to be developed from the detailed evaluation work done on the surviving strategy. In the long-range plan, resources are only quoted as ranges in each major category since the detailed program plans will examine the needs more closely and be better able to identify them. Since this is an iterative process, the results of the detailed program plans may modify the first statement of resource needs; any major modification suggested must be examined closely to see that it does not weaken the selected strategy. Also, few of the program plans will cover the full time period of the long-range plan, so their utilization of the stated resources, especially new working capital, must be less than the total assumed necessary for the whole long-range plan. The strategy to be used is obtained from the work described in chapter 6. This is the one part of the previous planning work that may need to be described in more detail, since some staff may not be aware of the details that went into its formulation and selection. Even so, the description should be brief.

The final part of making the long-range plan is to list the programs necessary to implement it. Several of these programs will have been identified when the strategy was evaluated. However, the full list must cover all the activities of the business so that the sum of the program plans is the company plan. Some program plans will refer to ongoing activities such as personnel, accounting, manufacturing, and so on. Others will refer to individual projects such as a new-product development or opening a new store.

It is not necessary to prepare complete pro-forma financial statements in the long-range plan. The financial objectives can be stated as ranges or limits for the parameters selected as important, for example ranges for revenue growth rate or earnings per share.

The final task of the long-range-planning exercise is to reconcile the discrepancies that will occur among the long-range plan, the program plans, and the annual plan. The decisions supporting the long-range plan usually outweigh those supporting the lesser plans, thus most changes will occur in the lesser plans during the reconciliation process. The long-range plan should be updated every year or when the strategy is changed.

One aspect that is not required in every long-range plan, but which must be considered very carefully when it is included, is planning for succession to the position of owner/CEO. Inevitably, there will be a change in strategy as a result of this event, but the current owner/CEO probably will wish to stick with current strategies. The long-range plan must consider the impact of succession and probable changes in strategy, accommodating them as gracefully as possible in the list of programs to be planned.

Program Planning

Responsibility for program plans should be divided among the individuals who will manage each program. The program plans for ongoing activities should be prepared for one-year periods to match the needs of the budgeting process. Treating these activities as programs is a type of zero-based budgeting since it requires a regular review of each activity. This is beneficial in ensuring that the business's operations are continuously upgraded to meet changing needs. The time period to be covered by the other program plans is, to a large extent, decided during the detailed planning process. Short programs (less than one year) to be started during the year must not be forgotten, otherwise the annual plan will contain errors.

If a company is already accustomed to strategic planning, the staff probably prepare strategic plans for each market served and for major products. Since these plans must be coordinated with the business unit's strategy, they are best regarded as program plans; the program is to improve the company's competitive position in the market, or to derive the greatest advantage from the product.

A program plan contains an explicit statement of a program's objectives and the person(s) responsible for achieving them. The plan also has a section relating the program to the company's objectives. The other major sections are similar to those found in any good business proposal:

the approach to achieving the objectives;

the major problems anticipated and comments on ways of handling them;

the resources needed, including personnel and equipment;

the program plan in any standard form such as a bar chart or critical-path chart;

contingency plans for unexpected problems; and

the cost, including levels of effort, staff, expenses, and capital expenditures, if any.

The cost elements will be used in the annual plan to develop the pro-forma statements of financial position. If the program plan covers a period longer than one year, these statements have to be divided into groups for each year covered. Program planning is performed whenever new programs are started, and every year the plans are updated to take into account changes in the long-range plan and to provide information for the annual budget.

It is helpful to assign priorities to the program plans so that the least important can be readily delayed or postponed if business conditions change dramatically. Also, some businesses may wish to add a few programs that can be started quickly if business conditions improve significantly.

Annual Planning (Budgeting)

Budgeting is an important means of planning, coordinating, monitoring, and controlling the business's operations. It may appear to play a small role in the strategic-planning process, coming right at the end, but this is not an accurate impression. The budget for the business is the most important day-to-day management tool. The strength of the strategic-planning process is that the budget is only prepared after the owner/CEO has determined which aspects of the business are the most important and which aspects need modification. A budget prepared on this basis is a more powerful management tool than one prepared as an extension of last year's performance with some hopes or guesses about what might be achievable in the coming year.

The budget should be prepared at lower levels in the organization, using information from the program plans. The managers who prepare it will have responsibility for implementing it, and if the program plans have been formulated and reviewed correctly, the budget plan submitted for review to the owner/CEO will be a realistic assessment of the financial activities of the company during the year. In most small companies, each manager will probably be directly responsible for the programs in his or her department, and combining the programs into a departmental budget will be straightforward. The departmental budgets are then combined at the next-highest management level and so on until the corporate budget is finished. The budget document is basically the pro-forma financial statements, with notes commenting on the major assumptions. However, for small businesses, the cash-flow and sources-and-applications-of-funds statements are the most important tools for management control to ensure continued operating strength throughout the year.

If a manager has to accept budget submissions from several persons, almost inevitably there will be differences to reconcile. But this should be easily accomplished as long as the planning schedule allows for it, and as long as meeting the corporate objectives is used as the criterion for decisions. The reconciliation process may require changes in one or more program plans. A good annual plan includes a contingency allowance for the unexpected things that can happen during a year.

The job of managers is made easier if the pro-forma accounts contain the previous year's actual figures as a guide and if the individual cost elements are also recorded as percentages of the totals. In this way, deviations from the plan can be identified more easily and the planned changes in performance from the previous year more readily indicated.

None of the plans are complete until they have been reviewed and approved at the highest levels in the company. Only the owner/CEO has the overview to ensure that the plans together represent the correct path for the business, and only the owner/CEO has the authority to approve plans that recommend deviations from standard corporate policies. Then the plans, or appropriate sections of them, should be communicated to everyone who has a need to know their contents so that the staff who must implement them know the chosen way and how it relates to the corporate objectives. Circulating the description of the company's business, the statement of business objectives, and the objectives of the major program plans to everyone is an effective way of informing the employees of the relationship of their work to the company welfare, improving morale as a result.

8

Implementation

"Time is what we want most, but what, alas! we use worst." —William Penn

Implementation Is the Key to Success

Strategic planning for small businesses is not performed outside the framework of the company or independently of personal needs. The whole process—planning, implementation, and operation of the company—is to satisfy personal needs in such a way that the ability of the business to continue operations in the presence of competitive changes and unpredictable environmental changes is optimized. Further, it is the process by which changes in personal needs are reflected in business operations, and the process by which the business adapts to changing external conditions. Preparing and implementing the strategic plan are integral parts of business operations.

Using the Plans

The completed plans can be used in the daily management of the business in several ways. One way is to communicate the company's objectives and programs to meet them to the staff. The individual staff members are better able to place their work in the context of the total operation of the company and gain a greater sense of participation; they also start to understand better the roles of others and see the value of individual contributions to the whole more clearly. Another way a strategic plan can be used is as a monitoring and control tool, with regular (usually monthly) reports on the status of individual programs and the current financial situation.

Many of the program reports can be done by exception; that is, the reports only discuss deviations between actual status and the plan. Financial reports should include absolute figures and deviations from the plan. In each case, major deviations must be examined and corrective action taken. Comparisons with the previous year's financial results should also be included. They help the manager study the interactions among the different elements. Since cash flow is the most stringent operating test for a small business, the financial reports must include cash-flow results and forecasts, including inventories and accounts receivable. Negative deviations from planned cash flow by a major program are a serious problem that must be investigated and corrected quickly. The reports should also include current data on manufacturing, selling, and overhead costs. Negative trends here cause concern too and need quick corrective action. Experienced staff members will recommend possible corrective action in their reports, and selecting the appropriate corrective action is facilitated by the existence of the plan and the supporting material.

Conflict Resolution

During the planning process, complex issues were encountered and resolved. The criteria used have value beyond the planning phase and can be applied to current conflicts. The owner/CEO and the senior executives and managers will find that the planning process aids their conflict-resolution process for day-to-day decision making because it provides lists of objectives in order of priority, decision-making criteria for many seemingly intractable problems, and experience in interacting with each other while they apply them. Adopting this management approach, namely referring to the strategic plan and its origins in order to support current decisions, ensures that the strategic approach becomes embedded in the company. However, the daily decision-making process should not be allowed to change the strategic plan. If major conflicts occur among parts of the plan, their resolution involves rethinking the relevant parts of the plan in the manner described, then modifying the operational plans appropriately to eliminate the conflict. Obviously, this can take time, but it is important to separate decisions with a long-term impact on the strategic plan from the hurly-burly of current operations. All the same, the real-life issues that arise during corporate operations are the ones that must be accounted for in the strategic plan by performing an objective analysis of the current situation in the company. Awareness of the types of problems that occur should be factored into the strategic planning process even if individually they are readily resolved.

Organizational Issues

During the implementation of the strategic plan, organizational and personnel issues will occur frequently. Many conflicts attributed to the plan are actually problems with the organization or personal rivalries. The strategic plan may require the organization of the company to be changed as part of its implementation, especially if there is more than one strategic business unit in the company. The contingency theory of organization states that the most important determining factor for a company's organization is its objectives. The objectives of two strategic business units must be different; if they are not, they should be merged. However, this is not the only factor. Two strategic units can be supported by the same administrative organization including personnel and accounting. Here, the value gained from maintaining the support functions in one unit outweighs any value gained by integrating them into one unit.

Not every organizational unit has to be a strategic business unit; some of the units have little or no contact with the outside world, earn no direct income, and trade with other parts of the business in account-book dollars. These units are cost centers. Their existence should be recognized in the strategic-planning process since their activities are important adjuncts to the revenue-generating activities. A good cost-center manager can increase corporate profitability dramatically by paying attention to the use of assets, the efficiency of operations, and cash flow.

The important requirements for senior managers are to ensure that the boundaries between the different organizational entities are clearly defined so that responsibility for operations can be unambiguously defined; and to establish policies and guidelines for the flow of data and information across the boundaries, and for the implementation of decisions that cut across the boundaries. Fortunately, in most small businesses complex organizations are not required. The owner/CEO should make changes where needed to improve the operation of the business and should seek an organization with integrity, where:

INTEGRITY = DEPENDABILITY + QUALITY + EFFICIENCY +
            FLEXIBILITY

The owner/CEO will appreciate the integrity of an organization when it exists even if it is difficult to define in advance or to order into existence. It is related to the integrity of the individuals in the organization but it transcends them; the strength of the whole is greater than the strength of the individuals because of the dependability of the organizational relationships, the quality of the organization's structure as measured by its appropriateness for the business, the efficiency of its operations independent of the people involved, and its flexibility to respond to new situations in a predictable, reliable manner.

Many other features of good management practice are reinforced by conscientious implementation of the strategic plan. Clearly stated objectives with clearly assigned responsibilities are generally regarded as important contributors to successful businesses. Good motivation of staff helps improve efficiency of operations. Good communications among employees, and between staff and management help higher-level control and decision making.

Management Styles

Questions. An effective management style is to ask questions that stimulate thought. Consultants learn many of these questions from clients over the years. What is your advantage? Do you have an unfair (unique) advantage? Would you put your money into it? Will you pay for the overrun in costs? Do you have the component (contract, check) in house? What is the first step? In an ideal world, what would you do? What change initiated by the competition frightens you most? What can the competition do to hurt you most? Why is that a straight line (usually referring to a projection of sales)? Why is it not a straight line (again referring to projections)? What happens next? How are you going to get there from here? What data (information, parts, resources, money) are missing? What does the customer need? Why are the customers buying elsewhere? What obstacles are preventing the customer from buying from you? How can they be removed? The answers to questions like these help identify problems quickly, diagnose causes, develop solutions, and recognize opportunities.

Lists. Another useful management style is to develop lists. They need not be formal lists, nor even distributed to other staff, but they help prepare the owner/CEO for problems. Which product specifications are vital for market acceptance? Which are important but not critical? Which are useful but not important? Which product specifications are the most difficult to achieve in development, or in manufacture? Are the vital specifications also difficult to achieve? If problems are encountered, which product specifications can be relieved with least penalty? What are the distinguishing features between a crisis and an inconvenience? Who would be first to be let go if business conditions turned difficult? The answers to these and similar questions are the basis for contingency plans.

Implementation Problems

Implementation problems appear in many different forms but conflicts of elements of the plans, staff, or organizational units are not among them. These are a natural result of human character, either the inability to produce a perfect plan or the inability to maintain smooth working relationships. A good strategy can help mitigate some of the age-old organizational conflicts such as marketing and sales versus manufacturing, or manufacturing versus research and development, or research and development versus marketing and sales. The plan helps coordinate their roles and helps the managers in each department make decisions using the same frame of reference.

Terminating a Business Activity

An organizational conflict that is a serious implementation problem is that between a department and the company. The winner has to be the company although the best way of resolving it is for both sides to address the causes of the disagreement and try to remove them rather than enter a win-or-lose fight. This type of problem can be exacerbated by strategic planning unless precautions are taken. It often originates from a strategic decision to restrict the growth of a particular product line or to withdraw from a market. In the latter case, the manager responsible for serving the market will almost certainly leave unless a challenging promotion can be offered. The owner/ CEO may not wish to see the person leave since the decision to leave the market was not necessarily a reflection on the performance of the manager. In the case of restricting the growth of a product line the manager may not leave, but resentment against the owner/CEO will almost certainly develop. Few managers enjoy being caretakers of a business while others are encouraged to expand their businesses and try new ideas.

Timing Problems

Other practical problems that occur during the implementation of a strategic plan are associated with the pace at which decisions are made and their implementation started. An aggressive management team can quickly outstrip the business's ability to respond to change. The problems can be as simple as out-of-date blueprints that are unintelligible to the production manager of the new plant, or as complex as inadequate training in the new products for sales engineers. If a company has been through some bad years, then maintenance, quality control, housekeeping, and training have usually been neglected. The facilities may just not be adequate to carry the load of expanded business activity. Presses that have been idle may not operate reliably, or the air conditioning might not tolerate more people in the office or two shifts in the factory. Financial controls may be almost nonexistent in parts of the company; purchase orders may be placed without checking the stockroom first, invoices delayed, and accounts receivable not attended to. Program planners need to respond to these and similar problems while developing their detailed plans.

A common problem faced during planning is the continual postponement of decisions until more information is available. The quantitative way to look at this is to try to calculate the value of perfect information, as shown in chapter 6. Even a crude estimate usually shows that it is not necessarily so valuable that continuous postponements are justified. The logical approach is to point out that no decision is actually a decision and it should be evaluated for effectiveness against the existing decision criteria as all the other decisions are. It will often be found wanting as a useful strategy.

Intended and Realized Strategies

The most formidable problem of all is the ad-hoc strategy. Business strategies form even without positive guidance (see chapter 5). The planning techniques discussed here are intended to create what Henry Mintzberg calls an *intended strategy*: an explicitly developed set of decisions for corporate operations supported by equally explicit guidelines for controlling the strategy over a period of years or until a major strategy revision is made.[1] This is strategy formulation. However, even in the presence of an intended strategy, realized strategies form; that is, a sequence of ad-hoc decisions are made, not necessarily by the owner/CEO, in response to environmental changes and operating problems. These decisions tend to reinforce one another and eventually form a clear pattern, the realized strategy. For some owner/CEOs, some of the time, a realized strategy can be an effective plan. However, its weaknesses include the facts that

it is not always created by the decisions of the people that should be leading the company;

it does not incorporate the personal factors specifically included here;

it is very difficult to communicate it to others to improve implementation because it is not necessarily fully understood;

it cannot be used to improve operational management decisions for the same reason; and

it is susceptible to exploitation by a competitor who realizes that it exists.

If a realized strategy is identified during the situation-analysis task, it can be very helpful in later stages of the planning process, especially during the strategy-formulation step, because there is no reason why the realized strategy should not be the basis of the intended strategy. Also, intended strategies can degrade into a modified realized strategy if vigilance is not maintained. There is a strong chance that this will happen if it is necessary to implement one or more of the contingency plans in a short period. Contingency plans have a habit of being self-fulfilling.

A final problem with realized strategies is the inability of an owner/CEO to see the need to change a winning strategy because of changes in the company or competitive environment. It feels safer to stay with the known and trusted way; it is difficult to advocate change if a strategy has served the company well. The existing strategy, intended or realized, is difficult to dislodge. This situation often occurs in industries subject to major technical innovations, in which products and services become obsolete quickly. Other common problems of technology management are:

> there are always more opportunities than resources to exploit them, so choosing the right ones can be very difficult; and

> the timing of the introduction of new technology is difficult. If a product is introduced too early, the company faces a major risk of over-reaching; if too late, the company faces major risks as the competition gains a market share.

Finally, the emphasis on programs to implement strategy may lead to an organization that adds programs incrementally, eventually losing overall efficiency. It is essential to control carefully the number of programs.

Continuity of the Planning Process

Maintaining continuity of the strategic-planning process is essential to derive the greatest benefits from it. The plans provide guidance, a framework for making decisions about new issues, and a method of monitoring progress. They are not rigid, and they are not automatic recipes for success. As a result, they should be modified when the competitive and general environments change. Also, the business operations should be changed where possible if deviations from the plan are identified. The only word of caution is that modifications should not be capricious; they should be evaluated against the current set of objectives and decision criteria before adopting them. If necessary, the objectives and decision criteria should be reviewed also.

The owner/CEO and staff have exerted considerable efforts to reach this stage of the strategic-planning process. Now they should start again. The process described here is not intended to be a self-contained exercise taking a few weeks and then ignored until next year. Many of the individual tasks are only performed annually, but the collection of data, information, and insights into the company's status, the markets and competition, and the environments is an ongoing process. The collection, analysis, and recording processes are eased by having the strategic-planning structure in place; the role and value of different pieces of information can be established quickly, and relations among apparently unrelated items identified.

Just as it is very valuable to continue the situation analysis throughout the year, it is also very valuable to continue to consider the personal and corporate objectives, the strategic logic, and other decision criteria, identifying discrepancies, opportunities and possible strategies. The greatest value from the strategic approach to business management is achieved when it becomes ingrained in daily operations. The preparation of an updated planning document may be an annual event but the work behind it is so closely related to the business that it should be performed all year.

Analysis and Synthesis

The planning process is demanding but it allows the owner/CEO to apply all the knowledge that can reasonably be gained to managing the business, which seems to be a reasonable action. Much of the process is analytical, examining and dissecting knowledge in more and more detail. In contrast, the important strategy-planning step is a synthetic process, putting knowledge together in a new way to make a plan. The owner/CEO can allow much of the analytical work to be done by others, except for the self-appraisal, for obvious reasons, but the synthetic planning task is much more difficult to delegate. It is more difficult to explain what is expected as a result, and to pass on the insights that enable a person to discern whether progress is being made in strategy formulation. One guideline: strategy planning should not replace common sense. Other guidelines will develop as experience is gained and the planning process is repeated.

Reviewing the Strategy Plan

The strategy plan should be evaluated annually and changes made where required. It should also be evaluated if major changes in circumstances occur: a death of a key participant in the process; an acquisition; or a major change in the economy for example. Finally, it should be evaluated about one-third of the way through the long-range planning cycle.

Personal Factors

Objectivity

The description of the planning process started with a discussion of personal needs and objectives, so it seems suitable to end the main discussion in the book with some more comments on the personal aspects of strategic planning. As always, objectivity in the process is essential, so it is helpful to consider some of the personal limitations that can cloud objectivity. All information we receive is immediately subjected to a sequence of tests:

Is it credible?

Is it relevant to our situation?

Is it important?

These tests are performed instantaneously and any piece of information failing one or more of them is likely to be rejected. Unfortunately, these tests are highly subjective and valuable information may be ignored because of this tendency to criticize it immediately. This is closely related to the discounting phenomenon discussed in chapter 3. The cautious planner does not discard information until it has been subjected to more stringent evaluations than snap judgments.

There is an extension of this problem. A marketing manager may recommend a new product but the recommendation may receive little consideration from the executives or the owner/CEO. They do not feel the suggestion has credibility and they have confirmed that feeling by asking themselves "is it credible?" to which the answer is inevitably "no." They just could not see themselves buying it so why should anyone else? In practice, that is a very good question and the marketing manager must have a good answer. Here, the sequence of tests can be used explicitly to check the credibility of the new product idea. This is a valuable use for the instincts of the planners.

Time Horizons

The impact of the time horizons of the planners on the planning process was discussed in chapter 5. It is valuable to remember that the people implementing the plan have individual time horizons too. They may well be puzzled by the reasons behind some decisions that cover a time period beyond their comfort factor. Also, there can be large differences between the time scale a decision is meant to cover and the time scale it is allowed to cover by the staff. A new procedure for handling product-pricing decisions may work well until a few weeks before the new catalog is published, when the staff may revert to the old way in order to deal with the overload.

The diffusion of decisions throughout the company is difficult to judge. The senior manager told the junior managers clearly what was expected of them but did the message get passed to the staff as clearly or at all? Balancing time horizons and time scales in the company is still easy in comparison to the situation when the complexities of the customers' time horizons are included. The owner/CEO is left to adopt a measured pace of decision making, informing staff and customers, and monitoring changes for some time to see they are continued. Otherwise, well thought-through decisions diffuse at an irregular rate through the company and the marketplace, eventually decaying toward zero impact as the staff and customers return to their normal practices.

Delegation of Responsibility

Unfortunately, this implies that the owner/CEO has to make every decision and see that it is carried out. If this is the only way the business can operate, it is in trouble. Delegation of decision making is still required. Handling the timing issues is a question of ensuring that the right tasks are delegated to the right people. If the owner/CEO has trained them well and sets a good example by handling his or her decisions professionally, delegation quickly proves to be the most effective way to expand the owner/CEO's span of influence and to keep up with a rapidly changing, complex business. The owner/CEO is now moving toward a leadership position in the business, and control of the business is exercised through a strategic plan formulated to satisfy his or her personal needs and objectives.

Value of Positive Attitudes

Finally, a reminder that strategic planning is not a barrier behind which owner/CEOs can hide. They must adopt a "can-do" spirit; they must have a positive attitude that objectives can be achieved in the face of problems. Necessity is a strong motivator, and the need to ensure continued survival of the business should motivate the planning process. Nevertheless, the owner/CEO must feel comfortable with the final plan (related again to the owner/CEO's risk tendencies). When the final planning decisions are made, qualitative issues will dominate despite the effort to quantify as much as possible and the owner/CEO's comfort factor will weigh those factors one way or another. This is fine as long as he or she realizes that is what happened—objectivity should continue to moderate subjective feelings.

Note

1. Henry Mintzberg, "Patterns in Strategy Formation," *Management Science* 24 (1978):934-948.

9 Summary

"The man with a new idea is a crank until the idea succeeds." —Mark Twain

Implementation is not the end of the strategic-planning process, it *is* the process. The first-time strategy planner will have severe doubts about the value of what appears to be a lot of extra work. The encouragement is that much of it is not extra work but a rearrangement of many tasks already performed; the tasks have been organized into a more efficient sequence with explicit recognition of a number of issues usually accorded little formal attention. The message of this book is that these issues—personal needs, personal objectives, personal attitudes toward risk, and compatible personal and corporate objectives—are critical in strategic planning for smaller businesses. This is contrary to current thinking in strategic planning for large businesses where rigor, objectivity, and analysis are regarded as the most important prerequisites for strategic planning. Smaller businesses need these elements too, after the self-appraisal has been completed. The close link between the persona of the owner/CEO and the small business means that the planning process has to start at the personal level.

This chapter first addresses the most critical aspects of the strategic-planning process which facilitate the process and increase the chances for ultimate success of the plan and the business. They are discussed in order of importance. It is interesting to note that the critical issues are mainly personal attitudes that can help advance the planning tasks, but the most important aspect for small businesses is the use of cash-flow projections as the evaluation tool to select the best strategy. The final section reviews the major steps of the process, emphasizing the linkages between them and the continuity of the process.

Cash-Flow Forecasts

Maintaining cash flow at acceptable levels is the most important feature of small-business operations. A good strategic plan provides the necessary guidance to the company to achieve corporate objectives and to respond to changes in the environments, but it will not be successful if it requires more cash than the company can provide from its operations, from new equity, or from new debt. Therefore, the most important evaluation criterion for

185

selecting among alternative strategies is the direct cash-flow test which measures the maximum amount of cash required to implement the strategy under consideration. In many small businesses, this requires reviewing the company's total cash-flow needs. But a quick test is to prepare a cash-flow forecast for each strategic program and examine the size of the cash investment necessary. If this looks reasonable, the full cash-flow forecast can be prepared as a final check.

The direct cash-flow test is preferred over discounted cash-flow techniques because it provides an immediate measure of cash needs unobscured by the discount factor. Since most small businesses will be concentrating on events over relatively short periods, up to eighteen months or two years, the direct cash-flow technique is a good measure of the situation. Discounted cash-flow techniques should be used, even by small businesses, to choose between two strategies that both pass the direct cash-flow test. Discounted cash-flow is an excellent way to determine which plan is the better investment, but it is not such a good measure of the financial resources needed by the company to implement the programs.

Effective Use of Time

The direct cash-flow test measures the financial strength of the company to continue operations. This strength will not be properly utilized if the owner/CEO and other executives do not have the time to prepare and implement adequate plans. The strategic-planning process cannot take so much time that it interferes with other tasks; if it does, or if the owner/CEO suspects that it will, little or no planning will be done. The best approach is to be patient and use what time is available for thinking and planning as constructively as possible. Many routine tasks can be changed slightly or at least viewed in a different light, to help the planning process. The secret is to understand the relationships among the planning tasks, and between planning and business operations so that accumulating information for the plan, and considering issues from the viewpoint of strategic planning becomes part of the continuing process of managing and operating the business. Accounting has to be done; sales have to be made; orders have to be processed; personnel have to be hired, trained, monitored, and reviewed; and investment decisions for new equipment or facilities have to be made. These are part of the normal operations of the business, so take advantage of them by putting them in a strategic-planning framework. In this way, time can be leveraged to the advantage of the planner.

Even so, there are some tasks included in the strategic-planning process that increase the normal workload; these include many of the personal tasks such as self-appraisal and analyzing the environments including the competition. No one responsible for an active business will find large blocks of time to address these issues; they have to be considered over a period of several weeks, perhaps months for the first-time planner, whenever a few minutes are available. A good strategic plan is very valuable but preparing it cannot stop company operations or soon there will be no business left to implement the plan.

The long-term solution is to take advantage of the plan, instruct others in the detailed operation of the business using the early plans as guidance, and free more time for in-depth planning. It is difficult to do this since it appears as if control is being relinquished; in fact, the owner/CEO's span of control is increased when this occurs but it is certainly counter to conventional intuition. The employees are implementing programs in a correlated manner and furthering the company's position without needing continuous monitoring by the owner/CEO.

Personal Issues

There are four personal issues that have a significant impact on the planning process and its outcome. They are compatibility between personal objectives and corporate objectives; objectivity; personal attitudes toward threats and opportunities; and comfort.

Compatibility between the owner/CEO's personal needs and those of the other important actors in the business on the one hand and the corporate objectives on the other hand, increases the satisfaction derived from the business and enhances the chances of success in achieving personal objectives through the success of the business. This is a fundamental philosophy of the planning technique discussed here. Of course, it is not essential to ensure business success, but it does greatly increase the chances that the personal benefits derived from the business repay the enormous sacrifices that must be made. Matching the two seems sensible, and planning to improve the match is rewarding both personally and financially.

Maintaining objectivity is an important part of later stages of the planning process, especially while performing the situation analysis and determining what can be achieved with the appropriate plan. Good ways to do this include conversations with competent outsiders such as professional advisors, members of trade associations, and other small-business people. However, there is a conflict between the need for objectivity and the need to adopt a "can-do" and "must-do" spirit. It is easy to use objectivity as an excuse for avoiding major challenges. The challenge may be a major threat to the business which requires a demanding plan to respond to it; the balance is between the damage to the business if the threat is not handled, and any damage to the business if the planned response is not completely successful. As long as contingency plans are included in the strategic plan, pursuing a demanding plan is usually the better approach. Necessity is an important motivator, and the plan should certainly reduce the damage from the threat even if it does not eliminate it entirely.

Few businesses will find life easy, and those that do are usually vulnerable to competitive actions. But the owner/CEO has the option of changing the business to ensure continuity of operations as long as he or she has the courage to do it. Similar dilemmas occur when a major opportunity arises. Are the rewards to be gained from succcessfully implementing a demanding strategic plan worth the risks involved? Personal risk tendencies play a major role in reaching this decision. An owner/CEO has to have confidence in his plan and the business's capabilities to implement it.

The final personal issue is the owner/CEO's comfort with the decisions made. Although we have emphasized the need to respond to challenges and opportunities with demanding plans, yet there will be occasions when the owner/CEO is faced with several options. If all else fails in trying to distinguish among them, he or she should choose the one that feels the most comfortable. Pursuing a demanding plan does not mean that the most demanding plan possible has to be created and implemented. This would be a failure in objectivity which can be balanced by remembering the comfort factor in making the final decision. Plans must be matched to threats and opportunities; too much self-confidence is as bad as too little.

The owner/CEO must also feel comfortable with the details of the strategic-planning process. Most people will modify it to suit their personal needs and this is to be encouraged. There are no rules and regulations that restrict strategic planning to one format or one class of problems. There is no recipe that guarantees success. The maxim is to recognize that activities in the company are controllable, and many activities outside the company are at least capable of influence if not control. Strategic planning suggests ways in which this can be achieved; ways based on the accumulated experience of many companies over the years. Many features of business activity have been identified as material, and the strategic-planning process presented in this book suggests one systematic way in which they can be utilized.

Overview of the Strategic-Planning Process

Figure 9-1 summarizes the main steps in the planning process. The objectives and decision criteria needed for successful planning are developed during the first tasks; they are passed on to later tasks for refinement and specialization to particular problems. The continuity of the process occurs when the detailed planning decisions and the results of corporate performance flow back to influence the original statements of objectives and decision criteria, which are then modified as necessary to start the next planning

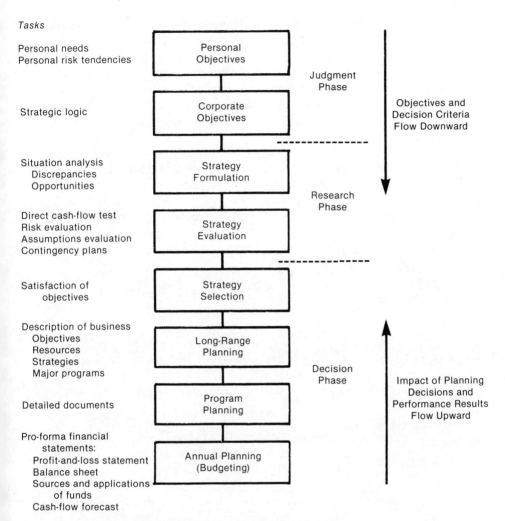

Figure 9-1. Summary of The Strategic-Planning Process for Smaller Businesses

cycle. The main activities of each planning task are shown in the figure; they change from personal and subjective to corporate and objective as we move from the beginning to the end of the process. Similarly, the time horizons shorten from the long range of personal and corporate objective-setting to the shorter view of the annual planning.

Strategic planning is the process by which a business prepares to achieve corporate objectives in the face of competition. The basic approach to maintaining the competitive position essential for success is to develop the strengths of the business so that they match the key success factors needed to serve the markets successfully, and array them against the perceived weaknesses of the competitors. The planning process includes organized decision making aimed at providing guidance for future operations and handling future events. The resulting strategic plan modifies business operations and repositions the company so that it is more likely to achieve the corporate objectives.

The benefits gained from a strategic plan differ from the benefits gained from an established planning process. A good strategic plan improves the chances of achieving corporate objectives. A good strategic-planning process means that the survival of the business, and the security and rewards for the owners and employees, are assured in the face of competition and changing environmental conditions, since a mechanism exists to respond to opportunities, threats, and changes that make the original plan obsolete.

Index

About the Author

David A. Curtis received the B.Sc. (Honours) in physics and the Ph.D. in applied physics from the University of Durham. He has also studied strategic planning with the faculty of Stanford University.

Dr. Curtis founded the management consulting group, David A. Curtis & Associates, in 1981. Previously, he was a vice president of Booz, Allen & Hamilton, Inc., in the firm's Technology Management Group, where he assisted in developing the firm's approach to technology strategy. He was also vice president in the Electronic Systems Section of Arthur D. Little, Inc.; a director of Cambridge Consultants, Ltd., in the United Kingdom; a lecturer in applied physics at the University of Durham; and a NATO research fellow in the Kamerlingh Onnes Laboratorium of the University of Leiden. He is a member of the Institute of Physics, the Institute of Electrical and Electronics Engineers, and the Project Management Institute.

Dr. Curtis is the author of about twenty publications including *The Economics of Office Automation* (1982), and *Magnetic Bubble Technology* (1973), and was a contributor in 1968 to the *Encyclopedia of Physics,* published in the Federal Republic of Germany.